LOCKE'S
SECOND TREATISE
OF GOVERNMENT

Continuum Reader's Guides

Continuum's *Reader's Guides* are clear, concise and accessible introductions to classic works of philosophy. Each book explores the major themes, historical and philosophical context and key passages of a major philosophical text, guiding the reader toward a thorough understanding of often demanding material. Ideal for undergraduate students, the guides provide an essential resource for anyone who needs to get to grips with a philosophical text.

Reader's Guides available from Continuum:

LOCKE'S
SECOND TREATISE OF GOVERNMENT
A Reader's Guide

PAUL KELLY

continuum

Continuum International Publishing Group
The Tower Building 80 Maiden Lane
11 York Road Suite 704
London SE1 7NX New York, NY 10038

www.continuumbooks.com

First published 2007

British Library Cataloguing-in-Publication Data
A catalogue record for this book is available from the British Library.

ISBN-10: HB: 0-8264-9265-7
PB: 0-8264-9266-5
ISBN-13: HB: 978-0-8264-9265-4
PB: 978-0-8264-9266-1

Library of Congress Cataloging-in-Publication Data
A catalog record for this book is available from the Library of Congress.

Typeset by Servis Filmsetting Ltd, Manchester
Printed and bound in Great Britain by MPG Books Ltd, Bodmin,
Cornwall

CONTENTS

KEY TEXT

Since the publication of Peter Laslett's edition of the *Two Treatises of Government* by Cambridge University Press in 1960 it has become the standard edition eclipsing all others. There remain many other contemporary editions that are all serviceable but all of which follow Laslett's example. From our point of view the detail of the *First Treatise* has been of marginal importance and some modern student versions still omit it. The absence of the *First Treatise* does not render all of Locke's arguments in the *Second Treatise* incomprehensible, but it can be misleading. The standard form of reference is to note which treatise and then provide the paragraph number rather than refer to the chapter or page numbers. Thus the famous discussion of private property can be found in *Second Treatise* §§ 25–51 (or II §§ 25–51).

CHAPTER 1

LOCKE'S *SECOND TREATISE* IN CONTEXT

i THE LIFE AND TIMES OF JOHN LOCKE

The author of 'An Essay Concerning the True Original, Extent and End of Civil Government', better known to successive generations as the *Second Treatise of Government*, was born on 29 August 1632 in Wrington in Somerset, in the English west country. John Locke has come to be identified as the most important English philosopher, as the founder of what has become known as British Empiricism, and among political philosophers he ranks as second only to Thomas Hobbes, with whom he is often linked in histories of political thinking, although the philosophical connections are at best contentious, and the personal connections were nonexistent. Locke's two great works, *An Essay Concerning Human Understanding* and the *Second Treatise of Government*, both published in 1689 (although written at different times), continue to merit discussion and debate as classics in their respective fields of philosophy. The *Essay* develops an empiricist theory of knowledge (epistemology) which is closely allied to the rise of the modern natural sciences at the beginning of the European Enlightenment. Locke's argument places epistemology at the centre of philosophy and establishes one of the paradigms of the nature and role of philosophical enquiry that is still with us. Locke's empiricism is often seen as the originator of what is called the 'under-labourer' view of philosophy. On this view philosophy is the servant of the natural sciences (which are the real sources of knowledge) by offering conceptual clarification and the justification and defence of canons of enquiry that are employed by the knowledge gathering empirical sciences. This conception of philosophy is much in evidence in contemporary analytical philosophy.

The *Second Treatise*, on the other hand, is concerned with the origin, extent and purpose of government. It combines speculative political science with a normative conception of the role of political philosophy as the legitimation of political power and sovereign authority. Rather than being an under-labourer for the practice of politics, Locke's conception of political philosophy is better seen as rational legislation, by defining and placing limits on what is and is not acceptable in political practice. He begins the *Second Treatise* with an account of individuals as free and equal moral subjects or persons bearing pre-political rights: even if they differ in terms of natural power, intelligence and skill, they remain equal in terms of their moral status. These subjects agree to the establishment and thus the limits of political authority as a response to the inconveniences of enforcing natural rights in a state of nature without a civil magistrate or institutions exercising political rule. He concludes with an account of the circumstances in which illegitimate political authority may be resisted, if necessary by the force of arms. This idea of government depending upon the consent of the governed and limited to the protection and enforcement of individual's civil interests has come to be seen as a paradigm for a constitutionally limited liberal state.[1] Although it is somewhat anachronistic to characterize Locke as a liberal in the contemporary sense of that term, it is undoubtedly the case that Locke's conception of politics and his ideal of individual rights and limited government continues to inform fundamental debates in contemporary political theory.

Despite sharing the same year of publication (1689, although the first edition of the *Essay* gives the publication date as 1690) Locke's relationship to both key texts is very different. Locke published the *Essay* under his own name and engaged in controversy with critics from its publication until his death in 1704. Locke's reputation in his own lifetime was closely tied to the reputation of his great work of empiricist epistemology. The story of Locke's relation to the *Second Treatise* is very different. Although Locke refers to the *Second Treatise* in his late correspondence, not least as one of the best discussions of the question of private property, he never publicly acknowledged authorship and resolutely defended his anonymity as author of the work. Many contemporaries suspected Locke as the author, and some may indeed have known, but he steadfastly refused to acknowledge the fact, except in a codicil to his will. We know for sure that John Locke was the author of the *Second Treatise*, but Locke made sure that none of his contemporaries could be certain. Why was Locke so reticent about the authorship of what is now regarded as one of the classics of Western political philosophy? The answer is complex and continues to be one of the main concerns of contemporary Locke scholars. There are two stories to be told about Locke, the first concerns the broader picture of his life and intellectual development. The second story concerns the specific political context of the writing of the *Second Treatise* and its crucial defence of a right of rebellion and resistance. Both stories are inter-connected, but it will be helpful for our purposes to look at them separately as the tone of the *Second Treatise* is undoubtedly shaped by the political engagements of its author during a certain period of his life. This political dimension to Locke's argument also partly explains the enduring interest of Locke's arguments to subsequent generations who want to place limits on the scope and exercise of legitimate political power. Before turning to the political context of the *Second Treatise*, let me say something about Locke's long and peculiarly eventful life (for a philosopher!).

Locke was born into the minor gentry, the son of an attorney of Puritan persuasion who served with the Parliamentary army in the English Civil War. Alexander Popham, the MP for Bath, com-manded Locke's father's regiment and it was through this associa-tion and as a reward for loyal service that the young Locke was able to attend Westminster School in London from 1647. After Westminster, at which Locke seems neither to have enjoyed himself nor excelled, he proceeded to Christ Church, Oxford, where he was elected to a studentship. During his time at Christ Church, Locke seems to have held fairly conservative views and wrote, though did not publish, two short works defending the civil magistrate's (king's) right to legislate concerning indifferent things (forms of behaviour that are neither required nor prohibited by divine law, such as stand-ing or kneeling, wearing vestments or hats in church, using images, statues, or even forms of address), issues that in Locke's day could (indeed often did) result in violent disagreement. The prevalence of 'Popish' or heretical practices proved a frequent cause for taking up arms against the ruler or particular minorities within the king's realm. It was after all only 27 years before Locke's birth that a group of Catholic gentry (that we would now call terrorists) had tried to assassinate the king and the aristocracy by blowing up Parliament, and within Locke's lifetime a king had been executed by a Puritan-dominated Parliament for disregarding the rights of Protestant Englishmen. In the face of such threats Locke appears in these early writings as a defender of order over dissent. More importantly, during Locke's time at Christ Church, he developed an interest in medicine and cultivating the company of natural scientists such as Robert Boyle, one of the founders of modern chemistry. Locke's interest in medicine and experimental science was to continue throughout his life and to shape the empiricist philosophy of his later *Essay Concerning Human Understanding*.

In 1666 Locke made the acquaintance of Anthony Ashley Cooper, the future Earl of Shaftesbury; it was a relationship that was to transform Locke's life and have a significant impact on Locke's politics. Locke took up residence at Shaftesbury's London home in 1667 and in 1668 he was to assist in an operation to drain an abscess on Shaftesbury's liver. This was a hugely dangerous operation in an age before anaesthesia or antiseptics. Miraculously Shaftesbury survived, a fact that he largely credited to Locke, but which may have had no connection with the operation. Following his recovery Shaftesbury involved Locke more closely in his political and commercial interests. Shaftesbury became the leader of the Whig faction in Parliament: those most hostile to the absolutist tendencies of Charles II and most fearful of the consequences of the succession of Charles' Catholic brother James, Duke of York (the future James II). As the conflict between Shaftesbury and Charles II developed, Locke decided to leave England for a tour of France. During this period he made a number of contacts and immersed himself in the philosophical debates between Cartesians (followers of the French philosopher René Descartes such as Nicholas Malebranche (1638–1715)) and their opponents. These debates were to have a further refining impact on his fundamental views on epistemology and the method and scope of philosophy.

Locke returned to England in 1679 just as the exclusion crisis was coming to a head. Following the hysteria created by Titus Oates' claims of a 'Popish Plot', the move to exclude the Catholic James, Duke of York from the succession to the throne led Shaftesbury to propose an Exclusion Bill in Parliament. Charles II responded to this threat by dissolving Parliament. In response to this Shaftesbury considered an insurrection. He was subsequently arrested, but due to the difficulties of securing an indictment he was released and fled to the Netherlands, where he died in 1683. Following Shaftesbury's death and the exposure of the Rye House Plot (an attempt to assassinate Charles and James on their return from the Newmarket races), Locke also fled to the Netherlands where he resided until 1689 and the success of William of Orange's expedition to remove James II and take the English throne as a Protestant king: what is often known as the Glorious Revolution of 1688 – it was in fact an invasion and conquest, however much subsequent apologists would claim otherwise. While in the Netherlands Locke continued work on the *Essay* and began work on a *Letter Concerning Toleration*, one of his most liberal works, which argued for a complete separation between politics and religion and also asserted the irrationality of religious persecution.

Locke returned to England in early 1689 and began preparing both the *Essay* and the *Two Treatises of Government* for publication, followed by the *Letter Concerning Toleration*. As has been mentioned, the *Essay* was published with a signed epistle to the reader, but the *Two Treatises* remained anonymous throughout Locke's lifetime.

Due in part to his association with Shaftesbury and his circle, Locke was clearly on the winning side in the struggle between the Whigs and the Stuart monarchy, and this is reflected in the last 14 years of Locke's life, which combines philosophical and theological controversy and debate with significant public service as an adviser to the Board of Trade and subsequently to the House of Commons on issues of currency reform. However, Locke had suffered from ill health for a long time (probably asthma) and in 1700 resigned his post at the Board of Trade and retired to Oates, the house of Sir Francis and Lady Masham, where he was to spend the rest of his life. Lady Damaris Masham was the daughter of Ralph Cudworth, the Cambridge Platonist philosopher, and she had been a long-standing friend and correspondent of Locke's. Locke continued to write, albeit increasingly on religious matters, but in 1704, after his health deteriorated further, Locke died. He is buried at High Laver in the county of Essex.

ii THE POLITICAL AND PHILOSOPHICAL CONTEXT OF THE *SECOND TREATISE*

Let us turn now to the context in which Locke composed the *Two Treatises of Government*. As we saw previously in the brief account of Locke's life, he wrote very little on politics until he became acquainted with Shaftesbury, and what he did write was both conventional and politically conservative. Following his association with Shaftesbury from 1667, Locke's involvement in politics and his political commitments changed. One of the earliest indications of a change in Locke's political views is illustrated by his unpublished *Essay on Toleration* of 1667. This work abandons his early authoritarianism and defends the idea of greater toleration of religious belief and practice, although it stops short of defending a right of resistance when the king oversteps his authority on matters of religious belief and practice.[2]

Locke's association with Shaftesbury undoubtedly brought him into contact with the political intrigues surrounding Shaftesbury's growing opposition to Charles II; this also contributed to the intellectual context in which the arguments of the *Two Treatises of Government* were composed. However the *Two Treatises* were not published until after the Glorious Revolution of 1688. It is still customary to see the *Two Treatises* as a vindication of the Revolution settlement and of the principles espoused by Shaftesbury who had died in exile in Amsterdam in 1683. Yet the Revolution settlement of 1688 and the re-establishment of a Protestant monarchy under William III is very different from the idea of a constitutionally limited government set out in the *Second Treatise*. So in order to understand what Locke was doing in writing the *Two Treatises*, why he wrote two and not a single continuous work, what is the relationship between the two works and why he published them anonymously when he did, we need to return to the intellectual context of their composition.

Peter Laslett (see Key Text) argues that Locke was working on ideas about the origin and nature of government in the late 1670s following his journey to France. The concern of these manuscripts was to challenge the idea of political absolutism which was clearly of considerable interest to Shaftesbury and the Whig opposition to Charles and his brother James, Duke of York. Some of this material forms part of what became the *Second Treatise*, which Laslett claims is logically prior to the *First Treatise*. The *First Treatise* was added between 1679 and 1681 following the publication in 1680 of Sir Robert Filmer's *Patriarcha* and a collection of Filmer's pamphlets in 1679. After the addition of the *First Treatise* Locke then completed the *Second Treatise*, which remained the definitive statement of his substantive theory. Filmer's *Patriarcha* posed a special problem for Locke because it offered a profound challenge to his conception of political rule as derived from an original contract and sustained by the free consent of all those subject to it.

Sir Robert Filmer's *Patriarcha* was written in 1653 as a contribution to debates surrounding the authority of Charles I in the period of the Civil War, but was only published in 1680 as a defence of Stuart absolutism. Filmer's importance is that he challenged the premises on which Locke hopes to build his political theory and defend Shaftesbury's rejection of Stuart absolutism. Where Locke begins with the premise that all men are born free and equal, Filmer denies this. Using arguments based on the Bible he argues that all mankind are not free and equal but born subject to authority. This authority is patriarchal, or a species of the authority exercised by parents. As all children are born subject to parental authority, all people cannot be free and equal, for children, even adult children, are naturally subject to the authority of their parents. This parental authority is then a species of patriarchal authority, or that exercised by the male heads of families. Such an argument would have been nothing but the most obvious common sense to Locke's contemporaries. Yet Filmer's genius is that he links this idea with that of monarchy by drawing on the idea of God's gift of dominion over the earth to Adam at the time of creation; this dominion is continued by Noah and his sons who became the inheritors of the earth following the flood. Noah divided the earth among his sons and then they repopulated the earth. Again this would have been familiar to Filmer's Christian audience. The sons of Noah become the sources of patriarchal power that has its ultimate origin in the original grant of dominion to Adam the first man. Monarchy is therefore an extension of this original form of political power granted to Adam. Two things follow from Filmer's argument: the first as we have seen concerns the origin of political rule, but the second concerns the nature of political rule. Patriarchs, like parents, exercise a complete authority over their children and most importantly exercise control of land and property. This latter feature of patriarchal rule has great significance for it means that all property relations within a monarch's realm are actually enjoyed at his discretion, as he ultimately owns his territory in the way in which a patriarch owns his land and property. Adam gives authority but also jurisdiction over territory to his successors. If the monarch is the ultimate owner of his domain then he can both confer and withdraw title to property to

8

and from his subjects. Consequently, he does not need to ask permission to tax his subjects, as he ultimately is the rightful owner of all property and land in his domain. One can see how the popularity of such a defence of absolutism would be of concern to Locke and Shaftesbury: not only would there be no case for limiting the authority of the monarch, but also no right of Parliament to withhold taxation.

Locke's response to Filmer in his *First Treatise* is to challenge the scriptural basis for a patriarchal conception of political power. By criticizing Filmer's interpretation of scripture, offering alternative readings that do not entail Filmer's conclusions, and inferring conclusions from Filmer's argument that undermine his defence of monarchy, Locke was offering a challenge to an important non-contractarian defender of absolutism. However, as Filmer's arguments are no longer worth serious attention, we might think we can dispense with them completely. According to Laslett, this would be a great mistake, for it is only by understanding the significance and detail of Filmer's challenge that we can understand Locke's alternative conception of political power and more importantly the centrality of the discussion of private property in Locke's *Second Treatise*. We can only make sense of Locke's actual arguments if we understand the positions he is trying to rebut, thus for Laslett we need to see the importance of the *First Treatise* to the *Second Treatise*.

The centrality of Filmer's challenge to Locke is widely accepted by all Locke scholars, but Laslett's dating of the composition of the *Two Treatises* has been challenged. The main plank of that challenge concerns Laslett's view that a good portion of the *Second Treatise* was composed prior to the *First Treatise* and that the *First Treatise* was composed following the publication of Filmer's *Patriarcha* in 1680. The debate turns on Laslett's view of the *Second Treatise* as essentially an 'exclusion' tract, that is a work written to support Shaftesbury's campaign in the later 1670s to have James, Duke of York, Charles II's Catholic brother, excluded from the line to the throne. Again this apparently small historical detail has a major impact on how we should read Locke's argument and why it took the form that it did, for it explains the appearance of a radically new dimension to Locke's ideas which is not intimated in earlier works, and that is the idea of a right of rebellion. Unlike other consent-based accounts of political obligation, Locke's *Second Treatise* addresses in a forthright fashion the problem of what should be done when the magistrate breaks the trust upon which authority depends. Far from arguing for an appeal to heaven and passivity which many contemporaries had fallen back upon, Locke argues for the right to rebel. However, he goes on to claim that it is the magistrate who is effectively rebelling and therefore it is acceptable for his subjects to resist him as if he were an unlawful aggressor.

This argument for a right to rebellion is important as it reflects the turn of opinion among Whig forces following Charles II's dissolution of the Oxford Parliament, the failure of Shaftesbury to achieve his Exclusion Bill and his subsequent arrest and flight to Amsterdam. Shaftesbury had begun to consider raising a rebellion against Charles II. And this strategy of resistance persisted after Shaftesbury's death with the Rye House Plot to assassinate Charles and James on their return from the Newmarket races. In defending a right to resistance in the *Second Treatise*, Locke is drawing a very specific implication from his account of political obligation based on consent that others had failed to draw, and one that is by no means logically entailed by his account of the origin of political authority. Equally he is aligning himself with other writers who believed that rebellion could indeed be a right and that government was not instituted by God and only accountable to him, as Filmer had argued.

But if Locke's argument is a response to the challenge of Filmer's patriarchalism and a defence of the right to resist, written at a time when resistance to Charles II was a serious possibility, why did Locke publish the *Two Treatises* in 1689, following the success of the Glorious Revolution? Conventional wisdom used to assert that Locke published his work as a statement and defence of the Revolution settlement. Most scholars now agree that Locke's intention in publishing the *Two Treatises* was very far from a simple endorsement of the Revolution settlement; indeed it was partly as a result of his dissatisfaction with the way things had turned out and this partly explains why the work was published anonymously. This is not to say he was unhappy with William of Orange ascending the throne as William III. What he was unhappy with was the speed with which the new authorities set about denying the revolutionary implications of 1688. Locke's argument in the *Second Treatise* is for a right to resist a magistrate who breached the fundamental trust of government and thus to re-establish a new government based on the consent of the people. Yet defenders of William began to argue that there was no revolution at all and no resistance either, for James II had merely vacated the throne by fleeing to France. In these circumstances William was able to 'inherit' the throne through marriage. So instead of a revolution that confirms sovereign power in the people we have a traditional account of hereditary monarchy, interrupted only by the inconvenience of James' abdication. Such a conservative justification of the new regime is obviously preferable to a monarch who does not wish to see his authority as conditional on the consent of the governed who retain a right to reject his authority in what they judge to be extreme circumstances. Far from being an endorsement of this conservative view of the events of 1688, Locke's argument in the *Second Treatise* is a radical challenge to it. His choice to publish the work in 1689 is a challenge to the conservative interpretation of events as little more than an orderly transfer of a vacant throne. Given how radically Locke challenged this view, it is no surprise that the *Two Treatises* was published anonymously and that he maintained that anonymity until his death.

In light of this discussion of the political and intellectual context of Locke's *Two Treatises*, we appear to have a vindication of the contextualist methodology that reduces the point of political theory to historical questions of authorial intention and meaning.[3] For the historical record does not only illuminate the interesting political developments of which Locke was a part, but it actually helps us identify the nature and meaning of Locke's arguments in the *Second Treatise*. Clearly, these historical readings have had an important impact on the way in which contemporary students and scholars have come to understand Locke. The question I want to finish this section with is whether such contextual methodologies exhaust the terrain of interpretation and whether there is anything left for philosophical analysis and criticism to do?

Historical and bibliographical study can and has always helped the distinct task of philosophical analysis and criticism by providing good authoritative texts and translations from which philosophers can work. Contextualist intellectual historians make a stronger claim, namely that the historical activity of recovering the identity and meaning of an argument leaves very little else to be said. What more, for example, can the political philosopher add once we have arrived at the appropriate historically authentic account of Locke's argument? One might respond by saying that the philosopher is concerned with analysing the arguments of past thinkers such as Locke, to see whether they are any good. By this one might mean whether those arguments are logically coherent, but also whether they are plausible; after all valid argument need not be true, and an invalid argument can still include true premises, and therefore be interesting even if invalid. If this is our philosophical response then we run up against the contextualist historian of ideas' assertion of the primacy of history over philosophy. For if we are concerned with plausibility or truth we must answer the question of plausibility to whom? If we are concerned with truth, then we must address the question of truth about what? Is there, for example, a set of perennial questions about politics that all of the great thinkers of political philosophy address and about which they can be right or wrong, or reveal more of the truth, than others? If not, what do we hope to learn from Locke's argument and from books such as this about his *Second Treatise*? If we find this quest for perennial truths a bit naive, as many in our historicist and relativist times will do, then we must address issues of plausibility and truth in a different way. Locke's argument must be judged plausible or true in relation to the particular historically contingent claims that he is actually making, and not in terms of ahistorical and universal criteria. A good example of what is at stake here is illustrated by the role of specifically Christian premises in Locke's argument. He can count on a shared assumption of the plausibility of at least some basic Christian beliefs amongst his intellectual peers in a way that no contemporary philosopher could.[4] This brings us back to the claims of the contextualist intellectual historian who argues that all of these questions are historical or require a historical answer and consequently there is nothing left for the philosopher to do.

All of these questions have an important bearing on what I am going to do in the remainder of this book. As will become clear in what follows, I will not be providing a historical reconstruction of Locke's argument and the context in which it was written. Instead I shall be concerned with the philosophical reconstruction, analysis and criticism of some of the most important arguments in Locke's *Second Treatise* and as mentioned earlier we will follow the usual practice (among philosophers) of largely ignoring the *First Treatise*. I will, where necessary, draw on historical scholarship to support the interpretations and analysis, but in so doing will merely follow the time-honoured practice of employing history to serve philosophical ends.

CHAPTER 2

OVERVIEW AND KEY THEMES

i THE *SECOND TREATISE* IN LOCKE'S PHILOSOPHY

Although political philosophers tend to regard the *Second Treatise* as Locke's most important work, many other philosophers would claim that accolade for *An Essay Concerning Human Understanding*, also published in 1689. This is undoubtedly one of the greatest works of philosophy written in English. It is also a major contribution to the European Enlightenment prompting a detailed response from Leibniz as well as inspiring an empiricist tradition in English-speaking philosophy that includes Berkeley, Hume and J. S. Mill, among others.

The *Essay* was begun during Locke's stay at Exeter House, the London home of the Earl of Shaftesbury, and circulated in a number of manuscript drafts, but was developed substantially during Locke's travels in France after 1675 when he immersed himself in the philosophical debates inspired by the work of Descartes. The ideas developed in the *Essay* grew out of interests in experimental science and medicine that Locke developed while at Christ Church and which originally drew him to the attention of Shaftesbury.

Locke's *Essay* defends an empiricist epistemology and conceives of the task of this philosophy as providing the foundations of experimental science. Whereas the emerging sciences provide us with knowledge about the world, Locke's philosophy supplements that substantive knowledge by exploring how we can have that knowledge or, more precisely, how it is possible for us the understand the world we inhabit. In order to explain understanding, Locke turns to the inner workings of the mind in thinking and reasoning and how that relates to the world that we think and reason about. His philosophy covers both epistemology (the nature and limits of knowledge) and ontology (or what there is). His philosophy is still subject to considerable debate, but it is also beautifully simple in outline. Locke argues that when we introspect, what we are immediately aware of is a realm of ideas, and he defines an idea as '. . . whatsoever is the Object of Understanding, when a man thinks' (*Essay* I.i.8). So our direct acquaintance is with ideas and not things. Ideas are seen to have two sources, either sensation or reflection. Sensation is the most basic form of experience where our interaction with objects in the world causes us through sight, sound, taste or touch to have ideas. Once that experience is written in the mind we can use or combine these ideas of experience in reflection and this is the second source of ideas. Ideas are also divided into two types, simple and complex. Simple ideas are either atomic (corpuscular) and might include such things as colour, shape and extension and taste, or complex such as when these simple ideas together give us the complex idea of an orange. He also famously distinguishes between the primary and secondary qualities of an object. The primary qualities such as size, mass and extension are mind-independent qualities of objects. However, such things as colour are considered to be secondary qualities given to them by experience. There remains considerable debate among Locke scholars as to whether secondary qualities are real, in the sense of being mind-independent or whether these are merely mental phenomena. Fortunately such debates need not concern us here. However, there is one important debate about Locke's theory of the understanding which does have implications for his political philosophy, although it is an issue he nowhere discusses in the *Two Treatises*.

As we have seen, Locke claims that the understanding is concerned with ideas and these have two sources, experience and reflection, the latter being ultimately dependent upon experience. The mind is effectively a blank sheet (or *tabula rasa*) on which experience writes. This means that there cannot be any innate ideas that we have *a priori* (or before experience) as part of a pre-programmed stock of knowledge. The idea of innate ideas might not seem so urgent to contemporary philosophers, but to many philosophers and theologians in Locke's day, innate ideas were essential for defending the truth of religion and morality. Many of the traditional arguments for the existence of God rely on *a priori* reasoning and an innate idea of a God that is potentially beyond experience and knowledge of whom cannot be derived from experience. To attack the existence of innate ideas was seen by many contemporaries as a direct assault on the rationality of religion. Clearly, Locke did not see his fundamental philosophy as undermining religion, for as we shall see he retained a strong commitment to the reasonableness of a Protestant version of Christianity until the end of his life. Yet the obvious implication of his epistemology for religion and morality was not lost on his contemporaries, and given the importance of theological premises in his *Second Treatise*, it has not been lost on recent Locke scholars. Peter Laslett goes so far as to claim that one of the reasons Locke refused to acknowledge authorship of the *Two Treatises*, despite avowing authorship of the *Essay*, was that he knew his readers would have seen the incompatibility between the two works and the extent to which the *Essay* undermined the basic premise of his political theory.[1] Locke, like most thinkers, was not fully consistent, and it is a mistake to expect coherence across such widely different works written for such different purposes: the question is how much we should read into these inconsistencies; were they merely the result of sloppy thinking or do they signify something more profound. Leo Strauss offers another more controversial reading of the relationship between the *Essay* and the *Two Treatises*. For Strauss, Locke like many other early Enlightenment thinkers is a closet atheist, for whom the anti-theistic implications of the *Essay* were his considered philosophical view.[2] Given that fact, Strauss claims that we must read the *Two Treatises* against the grain, and see them as a subtle and covert critique of the traditional doctrine of natural right. Locke knew that the arguments deployed in the *Second Treatise* could not withstand critical scrutiny in light of what he argues in the *Essay*. He would also have known that his more perceptive readers would have recognized this fatal tension and drawn the appropriate conclusions.

Strauss' argument is the most counter-intuitive interpretation of Locke available and therefore one I will not discuss further in any great detail, but both Strauss and Laslett in their different ways point to a problem in the relationship between the *Essay* and the *Two Treatises*. The argument of the *Essay* does raise serious problems for a defence of traditional natural law and natural rights, which we find underpinning the *Second Treatise*. This problem is the role played by the idea of God in the *Second Treatise* and the absence of God as a premise of the *Essay*. Locke thought that he could connect the arguments of the two works, although he may have failed to do so to his own satisfaction. We are less likely to agree with Locke's arguments, but the fact that he fails to achieve coherence between these works does not mean that the works are radically disconnected projects. The failure to achieve coherence is a failure: it is not a sign of the absence of any attempt to establish coherence. Jeremy Waldron is a recent scholar who has attempted to establish a connection between the argument of the *Essay* and the *Two Treatises*, as well as two other later works, *A Letter Concerning Toleration* and the *Reasonableness of Christianity*.[3] Waldron's case is that these works constitute a defence of fundamental or basic equality of a kind that is lacking in modern defences of liberal egalitarianism such as that of John Rawls or Ronald Dworkin. His case is not that Rawls and Dworkin fail to provide an adequately theistic defence of basic equality, although Waldron could be read that way; rather his point is that the structure of Locke's argument, including the way he deploys theistic premises, shows us the form an adequate defence of basic equality must take, and it is this which contemporary theories fail to provide. We will return to aspects of Waldron's argument in the next chapter. The plausibility of his argument depends on how one understands the final aspect of Locke's philosophy that I want to cover in this section, namely religion.

We have already seen that religious belief formed an important part of Locke's system of thought and debates about the role and claims of religion form an essential context for both his political and more general philosophy. The political problem of the *Second Treatise* and the later *A Letter Concerning Toleration* concerns the scope and legitimacy of political rule in the face of the claims of religion. Locke took religion very seriously both in his private life and publicly, and there is no reasonable evidence for the Straussian speculation that Locke was a closet atheist. Indeed he exempts atheism from toleration on the grounds that atheists must be nihilists who cannot keep promises or the obligations of morality. However, he also saw the problem of allowing the magistrate to impose religious beliefs on the grounds that this would cause (as it did in the English Civil War) political upheaval, but also on the grounds that persecution could not secure authentic belief. Authentic belief is important both for individual salvation (and what could be more important than that?) but it is also important because Locke appeals to the idea of a creator God to sustain his account of natural law and natural rights on which his whole political project depends. If his religious claims cannot be shown to be reasonable then his whole political philosophy collapses, hence the threat posed to his political philosophy by his empiricism. Furthermore, as contemporary students of political philosophy we might find Locke's reliance on religion and theistic premises deeply alien to the generally secular concern of analytical philosophy. If Locke's argument is indeed deeply imbued with traditional theistic premises then we might well conclude that there is not much to be learnt from Locke's argument, as the same fundamental questions about these theological foundations will keep coming up.

John Dunn has argued extensively that Locke deploys not only theological arguments, but arguments that are so distinctive of seventeenth-century English Protestantism that they consign his argument to the category of a historical curiosity that can have no political relevance today. Dunn is particularly dismissive of contemporary liberals who claim Locke as an inspiration for a constitutionally limited government. The problem then is not merely that Locke draws on theological premises, although that is difficult enough, but he draws on premises which we would now regard as narrow and fundamentalist. Dunn's reinterpretation of Locke is based on extensive knowledge of the details of Locke's works that do indeed convey a preoccupation with religious concerns and debates. Towards the end of Locke's life he devoted much of his time to defending the reasonableness of the Christian religion and to writing commentaries on the Letters of St Paul. Waldron, as we have seen, concedes much of Dunn's case about the role of Protestant Christianity in Locke's work; however, he rejects Dunn's conclusion that this renders Locke useless as a guide to our own political thinking. Instead Waldron suggests that Locke's appeal to religion provides us with an (though not necessarily the only) answer to the question of why we should regard every person as a moral equal. Contemporary egalitarians assume this premise of fundamental equality, but have next to nothing to say about why we should endorse this premise. Locke's appeal to religion shows why we should consider others as our moral equals, and the form such a fundamental justification should take. Yet where Dunn presents Locke's Christianity as a strange and alien world for us, Waldron takes a much more optimistic position by interpreting Locke as a more rationalistic Christian, who sees the fundamental compatibility between basic Christian doctrine and the claims of reason. Waldron's interpretation makes much of Locke's emphasis on the *reasonableness* of Christianity, where reason must be the ultimate test of revealed truth. Locke certainly did not see this concession to reason as quite as corrosive of traditional Christian doctrine as many of his contemporaries and as subsequent rationalist and empiricist philosophers have claimed. As a number of contemporary Locke scholars have argued, he was sympathetic to latitudinarianism – a highly tolerant and rationalistic form of Protestant Christianity – and towards the end of his life was suspected of both Socinianism and Unitarianism, which involves the denial of Christ's divinity and Christianity as a special revelation that overrides the claims of human reason.

We cannot hope to settle such complex interpretative questions about what were Locke's final considered views about the role of religion and the claims of reason in this book. What we will do in the next chapter is explore the role and extent of theistic premises in the structure of Locke's arguments in the *Second Treatise*. As a philosophical introduction to Locke's *Second Treatise* we have set ourselves an agenda of two main issues. The first concerns whether a free-standing philosophical interpretation of Locke's arguments can be distinguished from the social, political and intellectual context within which Locke was writing. The second issue running throughout this book is whether or not free-standing philosophical arguments can be distilled from Locke's other religious beliefs and commitments or whether, as both Dunn and Waldron claim in their different ways, the plausibility of Locke's arguments in the *Second Treatise* depends upon the plausibility of his understanding of the demands of Christianity. What I propose to show in the subsequent reconstruction and analysis of Locke's argument is that although theistic premises do play a role in Locke's argument he did not intend these to be 'confessional' beliefs of a particular form of religion. Indeed his reliance on a version of natural law as a law of reason was intended to provide reasons for those who did not and indeed could not have professed beliefs in Christian theological doctrines. Indeed as we shall see, what Locke thought he could derive from a minimal theistic premise was the idea of a rational created order. This idea of rationality could lead us to knowledge of the Christian revelation but it could also lead us to knowledge of the nature and limits of legitimate political power and the bases of political obligation. It is important to note that Locke saw both of these implications as distinct, although both rational. That at least will be the main interpretative conclusion of my account of Locke's argument in the *Second Treatise*.

ii KEY THEMES

We have spent a long time discussing Locke's life and context and some of the complex issues that surround how we should read the *Second Treatise*. These issues are important, as Locke's arguments have become a battleground in the history of political philosophy. In the subsequent chapter we leave those issues and turn our attention to the *Second Treatise* itself. We will examine and assess Locke's argument in a number of central areas. These are:

- Natural law and natural rights, including his account of basic equality and freedom
- The idea of slavery
- The nature, origins and distribution of private property
- The place of women and the family
- The origins of political society and Locke's contractarianism
- Consent and political obligation
- The right of resistance

We will explore the strengths and weaknesses of Locke's arguments drawing on the best current philosophical scholarship, including the work of Robert Nozick, Jeremy Waldron, David Lloyd-Thomas, G. A. Cohen and A. John Simmons. The key themes that are selected for discussion in the subsequent chapters are by no means exhaustive of all the arguments developed by Locke in his complex book. They are, however, the most distinctive arguments and those to which subsequent readers continue to return and in this respect at least they are classic arguments in political philosophy.

In the rest of the book we will explore in more detail the foundational values on which Locke's account of government and the state is based; the nature and sources of private property as a pre-political right; the origins of political society and Locke's answer to the anarchist challenge; his consent theory of political obligation; and his defence of a right to resistance.

We will not discuss Locke's influential theory of the state in the same detail, although we will provide an outline of Locke's arguments. This aspect of Locke's argument is extremely important but it has become an area where political philosophy has little to contribute and where we should properly look to constitutional theory and institutional political science. Locke did not have the advantage of being able to draw on modern political science to explore the best institutional mechanisms for holding power to account. As in this respect Locke's argument is instrumental we can leave its detailed assessment to one side and concentrate on the more important normative questions which still resonate in contemporary discussions of the basis of political obligation, the nature of and limits of state power, and whether if at all we have a right or duty to resist the claims of the state. It is to these questions that we now turn.

CHAPTER 3

READING THE TEXT

GETTING STARTED – THE PROBLEM OF ABSOLUTISM

For Locke the problem of absolutism was both a political problem and a theoretical problem. The Stuarts[1] believed that kings had a divine right to rule as they wished; indeed it was the duty of kings to rule free from the limits of any higher political authority. However, although the king could rule without consulting Parliament on matters of law and policy, he was obliged to ask Parliament for money, or new taxes. The Stuart monarchs sought ways of raising revenue without going to Parliament, as it would always place conditions on the vote of new taxes. This was especially problematic for a Catholic king such as James II with a Protestant parliament, but it was also a problem for Charles I and Charles II as both were suspected of Catholic and absolutist sympathies through their closeness to the French monarchy. In this context some defenders of monarchical absolutism argued that the king did not need the permission of Parliament to tax, as he was the rightful owner of his realm. This is the argument of Sir Robert Filmer's *Patriarcha*. As the king owned all property in his domain he could tax without consent – all the money was really his in the first place. Locke sought to challenge Filmer's theory with his new account of the origin of political power and the pre-political origin of private property.

Yet the problem of absolutism is not confined to 'divine right' theory. The English philosopher Thomas Hobbes (1588–1679) used a social contract argument to defend the position that sovereign political power must be absolute and unchallengeable, otherwise civility and the benefits derived from society would be impossible. Hobbes argued that even if we conceive of men as naturally free and equal such men would be obliged to give up their natural equality to an absolute sovereign. Absolute obedience to any effective sovereign power is a demand of reason. As Locke builds his challenge to absolutism on the basis of reason and agreement, he is by implication if not directly challenging the details of Hobbes' argument that social contract theory leads to political absolutism. At its most general, Locke's argument can be seen as steering between the false choice of absolutism or anarchism. As we shall see these two alternative challenges reappear in different ways throughout the *Second Treatise*.

From the First Treatise *to the* Second Treatise

Sir Robert Filmer had argued in *Patriarcha, or the Natural Power of Kings*[2] that all men are born into natural subjection and this is the lot of all mankind – sons to their fathers. Daughters are also subject to their fathers and women in general are subject to their fathers, husbands and eventually even their sons. Subjection and obedience to the monarch or political ruler is, for Filmer, just as natural. Obedience to the ruler is not an artificial relationship that we need philosophy to provide; instead it is the premise of social life. Filmer's argument is designed to show that such natural subjection is supported by scripture, thus supporting the idea that natural equality is not only 'unnatural' but also against the divine order. But Filmer is also concerned that the claim of natural equality will be used to justify the belief that the people have a right to resist and punish the Prince when they judge that he has transgressed the laws of the kingdom. As we shall see, this right to resist the Prince is precisely the conclusion that Locke defends at the end of the *Second Treatise* on the basis of our natural freedom and equality. If Locke did indeed begin the *Second Treatise* before the *First Treatise*, it is clear why Filmer's particular version of absolutism was of such interest to him.

Filmer's substantive argument about the naturalness of obedience posed a challenge that Locke needed to answer, but Filmer presented his argument in terms of scriptural authority, by attempting to show that political authority is a species of paternal or patriarchal authority that has its origin in God's donation of dominion over the whole world to Adam at the Creation. Locke's argument in the *First Treatise* is an extended analysis of Filmer's scriptural sources. Locke is concerned to criticize Filmer in his own terms and show either that the scriptural references on which Filmer builds do not support his argument or else that Filmer's interpretation is incoherent. One of the themes that underlay Locke's argument here and which he takes up in later works after the *Two Treatises* is that scriptural revelation has to be consistent with reason otherwise we would not be able to distinguish God's message from false claims to special revelation. So as well as interpreting the scriptural sources of Filmer's argument, Locke also makes rational arguments about inconsistency and contradiction. We do not need to spend much time on recounting Locke's rebuttal of Filmer, but I will summarize some of Locke's main points against him as these reflect themes that are central to the argument of the *Second Treatise*, and to which we shall return again. Locke helpfully provides a summary of his rejection in four brief numbered points in § 1.

Filmer's claim is that political or monarchical authority is established in the natural authority that Adam exercises over his children; consequently all political or monarchical authority is a species of paternal authority or more specifically patriarchal authority as is exercised by male parents. (Presumably Filmer would have regarded Elizabeth I as an honorary male!) Locke challenges Filmer's interpretation of the Genesis story by claiming that God's gift of dominion to Adam is unclear as it seems to involve both dominion over all things, i.e. property in the whole world, and sovereign rule over all people who are his progeny. These two types of authority are different, as we can see in the case of subsequent generations. Adam's dominion over the world can be inherited by his son in the way that property can be passed down through generations by inheritance. But this type of property relationship does not hold, according to Locke, with political authority. After all if political authority is a species of parental (patriarchal) power then it cannot be inherited as it can only be held and exercised by a parent. Parental authority must be re-established each generation and cannot therefore be inherited. So if Filmer is right about God's donation to Adam then political authority cannot be a species of paternal power. Furthermore, assuming that obligation to the monarch is a species of paternal power is incoherent. Does it mean that all parents, who must according to the book of Genesis be descendants of Adam, are kings? If not, how do we distinguish the real kings from the set of parents, as clearly this cannot be done by appealing to the original donation to Adam, and nor can it be done through the Commandment to honour one's father. Filmer's story is indeterminate on this count. Moreover, his theory also creates further paradoxes for it seems to suggest that not only does an original father enjoy dominion over his children, but also his remote posterity such as grandchildren and great-grandchildren. If this is so then it suggests that political authority is not a species of paternal authority at all for it is inconsistent with the parental authority eventually exercised by children over their children, and that it also conflicts with the clear scriptural injunction to honour one's father. God's donation of dominion to Adam does not create political power. What the complex scriptural exchanges of the *First Treatise* does is show that whatever else political authority is it is not a species of paternal authority.

In § 2 Locke extends the argument from Filmer's patriarchal version of absolutism to all absolutist accounts of political authority. Locke's claim is that absolutism in general collapses all forms of authority into political or monarchical authority. In Filmer's case all forms of authority are a species of male parental authority whereas in the case of Thomas Hobbes, who is not mentioned by name, all forms of authority derive from the sovereign authority of the monarch. Locke's point is to claim that these theories conflate different kinds of authority or power: he lists the powers exercised by a 'Magistrate over a Subject' a 'Father over his Children', a 'Master over his Servant', controversially from our perspective a 'Husband over his Wife' and equally controversially a 'Lord over his Slave'. Each of these distinctions collapses under the weight of absolutist claims that one particular relationship trumps that of all others as Hobbes claims, or that all are a species of one basic authority relationship as Filmer claims. Locke's claim is that we tend to distinguish a plurality of different relationships of authority or power on the grounds that they differ in kind. Consequently appealing to one kind – paternal power – will not explain the other kinds without begging the question. So what then is political authority? Locke's answer is given in § 3, which is important for the rest of his argument so I will quote it in full.

> *Political Power* then I take to be *a Right* of making Laws with Penalties of Death, and consequently all less Penalties, for the Regulating and Preserving of Property, and of employing the force of the Community, in the Execution of such Laws, and in the defence of the Common-wealth from Foreign Injury, and all this only for the Publick Good.

So political power or authority is connected to the idea of legislation and punishment for breaches of legislation, where that legislation is restricted to the preservation (not creation) of property and defence against foreign attack. Locke presents a very particular conception of the goal of politics. It is one that might well be very familiar in terms of the development of modern liberal democratic states, but it is by no means the only conception of politics found in the history of Western political thought – let alone beyond it.

What are we to make of this claim? Is it true by definition? Clearly Filmer would disagree, as indeed would Hobbes. Hobbes indeed might accept much of Locke's account as a substantive theory of political power; he would simply add that this is also something that is decided by the sovereign. The key point for Hobbes' account of political power and authority is that it is a question for the sovereign alone to decide the nature and scope of political authority. A Hobbesian sovereign need not be totalitarian and deny any distinction between politics and other spheres of civil society, but he must retain the right to judge the boundaries and extent of such spheres. Similarly Filmer acknowledges that the patriarchal conception of monarchy can allow for the delegation of power and authority.

Locke does not seem to be making a definitional move; indeed his more general philosophy would suggest a scepticism about trying to determine the nature and scope of political authority and power as a matter of definition. One way of making sense of Locke's claim is by comparing it with the recent claim of the American philosopher Robert Nozick in his book *Anarchy, State and Utopia* that 'Individuals have rights, and there are things no person or group may do to them (without violating their rights)'.[3] Many readers initially saw this as a bold first premise from which the rest of his book followed as a conclusion. But many subsequent readers have concluded that this is to get things the wrong way around and that this claim is not really the premise of his book at all; rather it is the conclusion that his subsequent arguments against Rawlsian distributive justice lead us to. I would contend that this is precisely what Locke is doing. The account of political power in § 3 is precisely the conclusion that Locke wishes to arrive at and is one which he develops in the subsequent chapters on the natural right to punish breaches of the law of nature, the pre-political nature of property and the limitation of legislation to the protection of a narrow conception of civil interests. Locke's definition will only be plausible if he can show the reasons for such a limited conception of political power, and this requires turning from definition to substantive argument and analysis. This argument and analysis begins unlike Filmer but like Hobbes, with an abstract (and not a scriptural) account of man's natural condition.

THE STATE OF NATURE

To explain the nature and origin of political power and authority Locke turned from Filmer's history derived from scripture, not to an alternative history, but to an alternative type of explanation provided by a State of Nature argument. Locke could have provided an alternative historical story, as although challenging the historical authority of scripture would have been controversial, and also something Locke would have been indisposed to do, there were many alternative historical narratives provided in ancient history or the 'Ancient Constitution' which could have served Locke's purpose. Appeals to an 'Ancient Constitution' were not uncommon in the period in which Locke wrote. This idea claimed that there was a longstanding constitution going back beyond the Norman Conquest of 1066 and which enshrined the true rights of Englishmen. Appealing to this idea allowed some of Locke's contemporaries to argue that the Stuart kings had overstepped their authority without having to construct abstract philosophical arguments from natural right or popular consent. The trouble with such arguments of course is that they, like the 'historical' argument of Genesis, are open to challenge and reinterpretation. Although Locke does not use such historical arguments as the basis of his account of political power he was certainly aware of them. Furthermore, as we shall see, Locke did not completely dispense with a historical dimension to his argument, but we may fairly infer from his failure to give primacy to such arguments that he thought they were insufficient. Instead Locke appealed to a State of Nature argument. This argument provides an account of a natural condition in which political power and authority does not exist and uses features of that condition to explain why it would nevertheless arise. Hobbes famously uses the idea of a State of Nature in which the '. . . life of man is solitary, poore, nasty brutish and short',[4] as the basis for his defence of an absolutist sovereign. Following Hobbes, State of Nature arguments have come to be a standard feature of social contract theories.

One of the most important features of State of Nature arguments is their abstractness. This has been one of the aspects of such arguments that subsequent critics have been most keen to criticize. Yet in fairness to Locke, abstraction is not a vice but a necessary component of analysis and explanation. The point is quite simple: we are asked to abstract away, or place in brackets, those aspects of our experience that involve the exercise of political power and authority and to see what we are left with and what precise features of that world might give us cause to create political power and authority. There are a number of qualifications we need to stress here. Firstly, the State of Nature argument is not simply an appeal to an abstract conception of human nature, although it does indeed involve such a conception; it must also give some idea of the circumstances in which that conception of human nature must act. Locke opens § 4 with the claim that 'To understand Political Power right, and derive it from its Original, we must consider what State all Men are naturally in'. If the argument were simply about human nature it would not provide an adequate explanation. Suppose Locke's argument was that all men are naturally selfish and egoistic (this is not actually Locke's view of human nature). What would follow from this? If we find ourselves with limited wants and considerable supply of those wants or material abundance then we might find that even egoistic people rarely if ever come into conflict about anything and consequently their condition is one of harmony – the spontaneous order that anarchist political philosophers believe in. If on the other hand these egoistic individuals find themselves in a world of scarcity they would come into conflict through competition for most things. Indeed this is precisely Hobbes' argument.

Locke's point in appealing to the State of Nature is to show how an account of human nature and circumstances create the need for political authority and power. Appealing to this device further suggests that political power and authority is artificial, or something that does not exist in nature but needs to be created. In this sense Locke is rejecting Aristotle's claim that man is by nature an animal who lives in a political community, and that political power and authority is natural. Locke's State of Nature argument certainly entails that we should regard political power as artificial and something that we would create (as artificers) if it did not already exist. But we must also be careful not to overemphasize this dimension of Locke's argument. After all, the device of abstraction is supposed to focus our attention on the nature and character of political power and to explain why it should be interpreted along the lines of the quotation from § 3; it is not designed to explain the story of the origin of political power: that would be a historical explanation, and as we have seen Locke is rejecting appeals to history to explain the nature of political power. His abstract State of Nature theory might then be perfectly consistent with historical explanations of particular states, kingdoms or monarchies. Indeed, as we shall see shortly, he does think that his philosophical account can be consistent with a historical or anthropological account of social institutions and practices. Yet he is making one very important point against the primacy of historical explanations, and this connects his choice of a philosophical method of abstraction and rational analysis with his rejection of Filmer's scriptural history. All such historical explanations involve a process of abstraction in identifying their object of enquiry. As such they are philosophical and abstract but disguise this under their apparent concern for the facts. This is precisely Locke's problem with Filmer's theory. He (Filmer) has a conception of politics as a species of patriarchal authority that he then traces back to Adam. However, for Locke, this so-called history begs the question, as it assumes what it purports to explain, namely the nature of political authority. The story of its source will not work as this assumes we know what it is and that is precisely what is at issue. The same problem would arise with appeals to the Ancient Constitution or any other historical narrative – they have the structure of explanation the wrong way around. Locke does not merely choose to attach priority to philosophical over historical explanations; his argument is that philosophical abstraction must be prior to any explanatory theory, and this view is supported by his account of the relationship of philosophy to the natural sciences which is developed in the *Essay Concerning Human Understanding* and which has had such an influence on subsequent conceptions of philosophy.

Locke's account of the character of the State of Nature identifies three important features that we will examine at some length as they are explained only briefly, despite being the framework for the rest of his argument in the *Second Treatise*. He claims that the State of Nature is a 'State of perfect Freedom' and that it is one in which people are free to act and dispose of their possessions 'within the bounds of the Law of Nature'. He then concludes that it is also a 'State of Equality'. Each of these features establishes an immediate contrast with that other great seventeenth-century contract theorist Thomas Hobbes. This may well be deliberate, as although Hobbes is not the direct target of Locke's argument his defence of absolutism is, so it is essential to show that in adopting features of the contract argument made infamous by Hobbes, Locke is not committing himself to anything that might entail absolutism.

Equality

Let us take the account of equality first, as this is central to Locke's argument and the first issue he deals with in his account of the State of Nature. What does Locke mean by claiming that men are naturally equal? His argument is very brief; indeed we might even claim that he provides no argument for equality, as he seems to rely largely on an extended quotation from Richard Hooker's *Of the Laws of Ecclesiastical Polity* (1594–7). Hooker (1554–1600) was an English Tudor theologian and one of the first to systematize the theology of the Church of England. Yet the quotation from Hooker and the brief statements of Locke's position in §§ 4–5 are extremely important to Locke's subsequent argument and reveal a number of important ideas.

The first point to note is that Locke is referring to equality in a particular normative sense. His claim is that in the natural condition all men are moral equals in that no one enjoys natural dominion or rule over another, so no one can be subject to another's will without a clear and unequivocal declaration that God wills it. This might seem to beg the question against Filmer but it is precisely what the argument of the *First Treatise* has shown – none of the apparent scriptural arguments for natural subjection are clear and unequivocal. As moral equals we are all equal under the moral law of nature; consequently we owe recognition of this equal moral status to others. This is where Locke's argument (and indeed that of all egalitarians up to the present day) becomes controversial. Why should the fact that I perceive myself as being free from natural subordination to another entail that I must extend the same consideration to others? Granting that recognition of moral or natural equality puts me under an obligation to respect others. Hobbes, for example, rejects the idea of a natural duty to others in the state of nature and instead argues that natural equality means simply rough equality of power, whereby the weak but cunning can pose as much of a threat to the physically strong as the strong can to the weak. This clearly is not Locke's position as his account of equality applies whatever we might feel about natural equality of power. Instead he uses the passage from Hooker to draw our attention to the idea of mutual respect and reciprocity that underpins the 'Golden Rule' that we should treat others as we wish to be treated. Firstly, we cannot consistently claim that others should love us if we are not prepared to love or treat them similarly, and further any claim that offences against our desires should be punished cannot be claimed if we do not extend the same concern to others. Secondly, it is in departing from this standard of equal treatment that our sentiments of injustice are aroused. Hooker's passage concludes with the idea that this equality is at the heart of the idea of law – the 'Rules and Canons, natural reason hath drawn for direction of Life'. Without equality the idea of law and moral rules makes no sense, as we would be faced with the arbitrary actions of individuals constantly in conflict. Locke does not explain or develop the point but he does suggest that fundamental equality must be at the heart of any account of law and morality.

Although Locke is undoubtedly right to suggest that equality plays some role in any viable account of morality and law, his argument cannot stop there as we need to say more about the group of equals. This might well seem an odd point but we must remember that Aristotle had argued in his account of justice in *Nicomachean Ethics* that equality should apply among equals and this was a group that excluded a large slave class and also women. In Locke's own day slavery was still an acceptable and growing commercial operation in British North American colonies. So it was not obvious that speaking of natural equality meant including all those we might include as equal persons. Furthermore, in our own day some philosophers such as Peter Singer argue that we must abandon 'speciesism' and include at least all higher mammals among the group deserving equal consideration.[5] Where and how does Locke draw the boundary of those who merit equal recognition? Many commentators tend to the view that Locke does not have much to say in defence of his account of fundamental equality; Jeremy Waldron has recently challenged that view in his book *God, Locke and Equality*. Waldron has a broader philosophical claim, namely that Locke can provide lessons to contemporary egalitarian philosophers about how they might defend their fundamental egalitarianism; we need not consider that. In what follows my argument will draw heavily on Waldron's reconstruction of Locke's defence of fundamental equality.[6]

In the *Second Treatise* Locke does use the idea of the human species as the principle of closure of his account of ethical significance – 'there being nothing more evident, than that Creatures of the same species and rank promiscuously born to all the same advantages of Nature, and use of the same faculties, should be equal one amongst another . . .' (§ 4). This claim runs counter to his rejection of species arguments found in the *Essay Concerning Human Understanding* on the grounds that they are nominal essences. Nominal essences are collections of ideas based on sensation and experience derived from nature. However, they are not based on real distinctions between objects of experience and therefore cannot provide the basis for real distinctions between species, and more importantly between mankind as a species and other kinds of species. The point about this is that our use of species terms cannot draw a real distinction between one species and another, although it can identify some natural features of creatures which are not shared by all. How we distinguish these criteria is largely based on convention and practice and it is for that reason that species terms will not provide the right kind of distinctions and discriminations. We can see an intimation here of the kind of arguments used by defenders of animal rights. Peter Singer would certainly not deny any differences between what we call species but, rather like Locke, would deny the significance of these basically conventional distinctions for real and morally relevant distinctions between classes of being. What we focus on in making such distinctions will draw the boundaries of moral significance and therefore who or what counts as an equal. Appealing to the idea of a common species will not do the relevant work because the classification is conventional though based in nature but it is not given directly by nature.

Yet according to Waldron, Locke does not assert the strong claim about species identity as the boundary marker of significance for the reasons he sets out in the *Essay*. Instead, he falls back on the less ambitious claim that the perceptible qualities that make up the nominal essence of the species Mankind do actually contain some real resemblances that allow us to draw a boundary around the group of equals as the group of all human beings. The key features that he picks out are that human beings are corporeal beings and that they have the capacity to think rationally or (what he takes to be the same thing) abstractly. The emphasis on corporeal (embodied) beings is important because it suggests that Locke is concerned with human selves or persons and not souls despite his obvious religious commitments. This criterion distinguishes human persons from any other kind of non-corporeal entity should they exist and whatever they might happen to be.

The second characteristic that Locke identifies is the capacity for abstract thought or rationality. This immediately suggests one standard objection to all naturalistic attempts to ground ethical equality, namely that not all of those we might include among 'humankind' express the capacity to think abstractly. One simple response would be to robustly deny that those who do not manifest that characteristic are moral equals. Thus infants, most children up to a certain age, many elderly people as well as those with mental disabilities, those in comas, etc. would seem to fall outside the scope of moral equality. And many of Locke's contemporaries would have made similar claims about women as less than rational beings. Locke does not take this view; instead, according to Waldron, he uses the capacity to exhibit abstract rational thought as a range-property (an idea Waldron derives from the contemporary philosopher John Rawls) which seems to fit Locke's arguments about the scope of the capacity for abstract thought. The point about a range-property is that it allows for differences of degree within a range. Waldron illustrates the point with the example of being in New Jersey. Both Hoboken and Princeton fall within the range concept though they differ in the degree to which they fall within the State of New Jersey. Hoboken is on the border with New York. It is falling within the range that matters and not the degree. So although people differ in the degree to which they exhibit the capacity for abstract thought, this does not matter from the point of view of identifying the relevant criterion of equality.

But even if we can use the idea of the capacity for abstract thought among corporeal beings, the argument seems to fall foul of the other standard criticism of naturalistic theories of ethics, namely how ethical significance is derived from what Locke concedes is a natural capacity, or how we move from descriptive to prescriptive equality. It is here that Locke's argument for equality connects with his account of the source of ethical significance, namely God.

The argument works in the following way: the capacity of abstract reasoning is identified as significant, not simply because it is widely or universally shared (though to differing degrees) by all human beings. Instead the significance of abstract reasoning is that it enables each person to understand themselves as a part of the created order and from this they can reason to their obligation to preserve that order including other moral equals as part of the basic moral obligation we have to God. This is further illustrated by Locke's use of the quotation from Hooker. We will return to this point shortly when we look at Locke's defence of the law of nature. But there remains one important point that we can derive from Waldron's interpretation, and that is that Locke's appeal to God is not simply for the traditional natural law idea of an authoritative sanction of our basic moral obligation. Clearly, for Locke, God does sanction the basic moral law of equal respect, but that is not the key point. As we shall see later Locke's account of law is not a simple voluntarist theory whereby law is based on the will of the lawgiver – once again this is a clear distinction between Hobbes and Locke. Instead the appeal to God, and therefore a transcendent authority, provides the meaning and significance of the real resemblances (corporeality and capacity for rationality) on which moral equality is based.

Freedom

We have spent a lot of time on Locke's account of fundamental equality and as we proceed through his text we will see the continuing significance of that commitment. But equality is not the only fundamental value that we find in Locke's characterization of the State of Nature. Locke also describes the State of Nature as a 'State of perfect Freedom'. The conception of Freedom is clarified in § 6 where Locke draws an important distinction between a 'State of Liberty' and a 'State of Licence'. Once again this distinction separates Locke's argument from predecessors such as Hobbes and successor such as Bentham or Mill. We can explain this distinction by drawing on Isaiah Berlin's famous distinction between negative and positive freedom.[7] On the negative concept of freedom an agent is free when she is not restricted from acting. Berlin goes on to qualify that claim by exploring the nature of restrictions. Is a physical inability a restriction in the relevant sense? Would I be unfree because my inability restricts me from jumping over the moon? Similarly, if I have a strong psychological aversion to doing something am I therefore unfree? Is a Jew or a Muslim 'unfree' to eat pork, because she has a strong religiously based aversion to so doing? Berlin's argument tends towards only allowing external restrictions as limitations on freedom. Thus the Jew or Muslim would be free to eat pork just as a Catholic woman would be free to have an abortion, as long as they are not prevented by the actions of others from doing so. They would be unfree if the state prevented them from buying pork or obtaining an abortion, even if they would never choose to do so. These external restrictions on action also have to be of a certain kind; The absence of resources is not an external restriction of the relevant kind, consequently one is not unfree to eat at the best restaurant simply because one cannot afford to. The relevant class of restrictions are derived from the actions of others. Thus I am not unfree to jump over the moon, I am simply unable to do so. An inability is not a restriction because it does not involve the interference of another agent. The negative liberty account of restrictions is potentially complicated by the introduction of the issue of threats. If I do not stop you doing something but give you a reason not to do something through fear of a later action by me, do I limit your freedom? If I threaten to set my dog on you if you walk on my lawn, do I thereby limit your freedom to walk on my lawn? This issue of threats is important as it connects with the issue of how law might restrict freedom. Clearly laws put up barriers to acting in many ways and therefore can appear to restrict freedom, but much of the time the law does not actually stop you doing something, it merely states (threatens) consequences if you so act. Property laws do not stop burglars burgling houses, but they do threaten consequences if burglars ignore the rights of property under law. These challenges and distinctions are at the heart of Locke's account of freedom in the State of Nature.

As we have seen, Locke rejects the idea that our freedom consists of the unrestricted pursuit of our wants and desires. In this he draws a further contrast between his account of the State of Nature and that which we find in Hobbes. For Hobbes, in the State of Nature we have an unrestricted (subjective) right to whatever we need to preserve ourselves, up to and including the body of another. By this he means we are under no obligation not to kill another person if they threaten our life and preservation. For Hobbes, freedom consists of the absence of restrictions on our actions by other people. On the negative view of liberty, freedom is merely a descriptive category. One can be free to do things which are repugnant (murder, etc.) without the negative liberty theorist having to say that these actions are good. Indeed Hobbes thought that freedom was a problem. His is a classic defence of negative freedom and one of the main bases of Berlin's distinction. Locke on the other hand would regard such an account of liberty as mere licence and contrast it with true freedom.

For Locke, in contrast to Hobbes, we are not free to kill ourselves or to kill others, and this is not merely because we are physically prevented from doing so, but because we have no right to do so. Rights and their concomitant duties place restrictions on what we may legitimately do, but that according to Locke does not mean that they restrict our freedom or liberty. Instead the Law of Nature that distributes rights and duties actually constitutes our freedom or liberty. In Locke's sense, liberty is a fundamentally normative concept that can only be explained in relation to a moral rule or law. In this respect Locke might be considered to have a positive conception of freedom, according to Berlin's distinction, because to be free for Locke consists in acting in a particular way and not simply following our whims and doing what we wish. When we act against the Law of Nature we are not acting freely. This is so even in the State of Nature where there is no authority that imposes a law and guarantees its enforcement. Locke's point is that freedom is clearly a moral concept and that it does not make sense for him to say one acted freely but wrongly, or that freedom might be undesirable – as indeed Hobbes thought.

Defenders of the negative concept of liberty would justify their position by saying that Locke is confusing two different concepts such as freedom and justice whereas we must distinguish different values and moral goals and recognize that they can conflict. Contemporary critics of the negative or descriptive approach to freedom claim that it can result in counter-intuitive consequences. We might for example argue on the negative view that North Korea is more free than Britain or the USA on the grounds that there are far fewer traffic laws, building regulations and consumer protection laws in North Korea. In North Korea we might argue there are only three main restrictions – to engage in political activity, to speak freely and to practise religion. For Locke such a conclusion would be absurd. It is not the number of restrictions that matters but the nature and character of those restrictions, and to make sense of these we need to turn to his account of the Law of Nature, which distinguishes liberty from licence.

The Law of Nature

The *State of Nature* has a Law of Nature to govern it, which obliges every one: And Reason, which is that Law, teaches all Mankind, who will but consult it, that being equal and independent, no one ought to harm another in his Life, Health, Liberty or Possessions. (§ 6)

Into this short passage Locke distils the foundation and substance of his political philosophy. The State of Nature is not a war of all against all but is law governed and that law is the source of obligations and rights. Locke packs a lot into a short section of the *Second Treatise* so we need to be careful in drawing out the full implications of what he says. Let us begin with the formal features of his account of the Law of Nature.

First, the Law of Nature is a law and it obliges people by creating obligations. This is important as a contrast with Hobbes, who used the idea of the Law of Nature in the State of Nature as a shorthand for prudential advice. Laws of Nature in that sense are akin to generalizations from what people want or are inclined to do. For Locke, law is different in that it tells us what we ought to do – law is normative and not descriptive. What follows from this claim is that the Law of Nature is distinct from and logically prior to any positive laws and conventional moral and social rules or moral beliefs that people hold at particular times and places. Positive laws are those laws that claim as their authority the fact that they have been made by legislative institutions such as Parliament or Congress. By claiming that the Law of Nature holds in the State of Nature, Locke is clear in defending the idea that the source of normativity or our most basic obligations is pre-political and pre-conventional. An immediate consequence of this is that positive or conventional laws and moral rules are only legitimate and binding in so far as they are derivable or consistent with the Law of Nature. Kings, princes and legislatures are therefore just as much bound by the Law of Nature as anyone else, as we shall see later; this is the most important claim of Locke's argument – all human legislatures or rulers are bound by this higher law. The Law of Nature is also logically prior to any conventional or positive laws, because it is that which explains why these conventional and positive laws might be binding. If we are simply left with conventions, where law is just what a legislative institution says it is, or a moral rule is simply 'how we do things around here', one might well argue 'So what?' If conventions seem foolish or wrong, or the legislature prescribes things that contradict my moral beliefs, I might well claim that in the clash of mere beliefs, mine are as good as anyone else's. This attitude leads to anarchy, but rather than simply arguing that I must conform because anarchy is costly, painful and inconvenient, Locke provides an external criterion for assessing what can count as a law and therefore provides an answer to my sceptical query that does not boil down to 'this is just how we do things around here'.

Secondly, Locke identifies the Law of Nature with a Law of Reason. We can know what the law is by exercising our faculty of reason. In this claim Locke follows a long tradition of philosophy that goes back to the Stoics in Roman times, as it is here that we first see reason as a source of law. As we saw in the discussion of fundamental equality the capacity of reason leads us to knowledge of God, but it is important to note that Locke's claim is that the authority of law even if from God must come through reason first and foremost. Reason is the capacity we use to know that there is a God, and as this is something that is important for all men (and women) in whatever age and whatever place, our knowledge of God and the commands of his law cannot be derived from the Bible, scripture or special revelation. If knowledge of the Law of Nature was only derivable from the Bible, it would not be available to all those men and women in parts of the world who have no knowledge of it. This would be profoundly unfair as it would place men under obligations for which they would be subject to punishment in the event of non-compliance, which they could not know about. So the Law of Nature must not only be universally binding, but it must be universally knowable. That Locke agonized over the relationship between reason and revelation is illustrated by many of his later works such as *The Reasonableness of Christianity* where he tries to describe the rational core of Christianity.

However, Locke's appeal to reason as the source of our knowledge of God becomes problematic, as in one of his other great works, *Essay Concerning Human Understanding*, he argues that all our knowledge comes from experience. The problem is that our experience does not necessarily lead to an experience of God. As many in our own time as much as in Locke's are only too quick to claim, experience undermines any possibility of knowing God. Later critics of revealed and natural religion, such as the Scottish philosopher David Hume (1711–76), used a similar epistemology to draw profoundly sceptical conclusions. Some subsequent Locke scholars have also claimed that Locke's awareness of the incompatibility of the two arguments partly caused Locke to deny authorship of the *Second Treatise*, for fear that his own epistemological arguments could be turned against his defence of the Law of Nature. Some scholars have gone even further, claiming that Locke's argument in the *Second Treatise* was a deliberate sham as he was an atheist, as evidenced by his epistemology.

But we seem to be getting ahead of ourselves for we have moved quickly from the Law of Nature as a Law of Reason to discussion of the role of reason in leading us to a knowledge of God. To see why this issue arises we need to turn from the formal features of the idea of a Law of Nature to the substance of Locke's account of the fundamental Law of Nature. As we have seen, Locke claims that the Law of Nature obligates mankind not to harm each other in the enjoyment of 'Life, Health, Liberty or Possessions'. Later in § 7 he goes further and claims that 'the Law of Nature . . . willeth the Peace and *Preservation of all Mankind*'. It is this latter idea that connects the Law or Nature with the role of God. Why is it that we should preserve ourselves and preserve all mankind? The answer is simple, albeit controversial: 'For Men being all the Workmanship of one Omnipotent and infinitely wise Maker . . . they are his Property, whose Workmanship they are, made to last during his, not anothers Pleasure'. The theological premise in Locke's argument is that God made us and therefore we are his property and should exist at his discretion, not that of anyone else. He made us; he owns us.

Self-preservation, for Locke, is not merely an empirical generalization from people's fear of a violent death as Hobbes claimed. This sort of argument would not work, as many people – suicide bombers, gang members, or courageous soldiers in battle – do not fear a violent death. Yet according to Locke, we are under a strict moral duty to preserve ourselves. Why should we acknowledge such a duty? Locke's argument falls back onto a theological premise, but one he thinks it is reasonable for all men to accept. We can, for example, know that there is a Creator God because there is a created order – a world for us to see and experience. Because there is something and not nothing, there must have been a Creator who brought that order into existence. So reason takes us to knowledge of God, but only in this special sense of God as a Creator. We are not required to believe anything else about God's nature and his actions or non-actions in the world. This claim of reason does not provide us with knowledge of a specifically Christian, Jewish or Muslim God. The question we are left with is whether this argument is quite as minimal as Locke thinks. There are at least two problems that I will outline but not attempt to resolve, one of which we will return to in the discussion of Locke on property in Chapter V.

Locke's argument depends upon the claim, although he does not state it as such, that we can infer the idea of a Creator God from the direct and uncontroversial experience of a created order. But is this sufficient? We might, following sceptical critics of Locke, infer from our experience that the world always existed and was not created. There is no obvious reason that the idea of an eternal world is any less an obvious inference than the idea of an eternal Creator God. Furthermore, even if we do accept the inference from creation to Creator, we might just as legitimately infer that there was once a Creator or first cause who initiated the universe but who then ceased to exist and left an impersonal mechanism after him. This conclusion would be problematic for Locke, because it would free us from being the property of someone even though we might still be his workmanship. We can draw out the analogy by thinking of a piece of art produced by an artist who then dies, without leaving a will or without selling the work to a third party. In this case the work would be workmanship but not property in the sense that anyone could lay a claim of ownership over it. If that is the case we face the problem of justifying the restrictions that Locke thinks follow from his account of mankind as God's workmanship. Contrary to the interpretation of contemporary political philosophers such as Nozick, Locke does not provide what is called a 'self-ownership' argument. The 'self-ownership' argument claims that we have full property in our person and body because no one else owns us. But one consequence of this is that Nozick allows that we can sell ourselves into slavery and that we have a right to commit suicide.

It is clear that Locke denies that we have any such right to commit suicide, as the whole point of the argument that we are God's workmanship is that we exist at his pleasure and not our own. Thus we have a duty to preserve ourselves by eating and staying healthy as far as possible and not killing ourselves. Certainly, Locke accepts that because we are ultimately God's property we cannot be owned by anyone else, and this creates a kind of 'property' over our bodies. But the analogy here would be that we at best enjoy a leasehold right over our bodies whereas God retains the freehold. We certainly do not have what many claim is central to the idea of a full property right, namely the right to destroy the thing owned.

If we acknowledge that the argument from God as a Creator is weak then Locke's argument ends up as precarious as Nozick's contemporary argument, with the source of the duty of preservation of ourselves and others remaining mysterious. We might claim that we just have a psychological propensity to seek preservation, but this might not apply in all cases, as we have seen, and it certainly gives us no reason to be concerned about the preservation of others. All of this is not to concede that Locke is wrong, as he still has some contemporary defenders of his minimal rational theological claims, such as Forster.[8]

A further problem for Locke is why the act of creation creates a right in the thing created? We will return to this question in the discussion of private property, but it is worth noting that it applies just as much to God's relationship with his workmanship as it does in relation to man and the products of his labour. So even if we overcome all the problems of knowledge of God and his persistence in order to claim his right, we still have a question concerning how creation establishes claims of ownership. Perhaps Locke's discussion of private property will provide the support for the argument sketched out in these sections. What is not developed anywhere else in this work, but was something that preoccupied Locke throughout much of his later career, was addressing the sceptical challenge to the existence and nature of God. Let us leave that issue and turn to the further formal dimension of Locke's account of the Law of Nature.

Right and duty to punish – Executive power of the Law of Nature

One very important feature of Locke's account of the Law of Nature is that it is genuinely a law and not merely a rational principle or belief about what we should do. Locke's theory of law is not a crude voluntarist theory, whereby a law is simply the expression of the will of a lawgiver backed by a sanction or punishment. As we have just seen, the Law of Nature is supposed to contain a rational content, but it must also be a sanctioned reason, one for which non-compliance merits punishment. Law and punishment go together. Now one might think that after the introduction of God into his account of the substance of the Law of Nature, Locke merely relies on the threat of eternal punishment or reward as the sanctions of his theory. In this way God sanctions his law but the punishment is deferred to a later time, after our deaths and at the Judgement. But this can neither be Locke's argument nor is it. First, it cannot be, as the inference from creation to a Creator God gives us no similar inference to divine reward and punishment or heaven and hell. Even if the idea of God is a precondition of his creation, hell is not. Yet more than this, Locke also claims that the Law of Nature is complete in the State of Nature, it is a real law and not an indication of a law, and that is because it has a real and legitimate sanction in the Law of Nature. He claims '. . . the *Law of Nature* would . . . be in vain, if there were no body that in the State of Nature, had the *Power to Execute* that Law . . .' (§ 7). Locke's argument is that everyone in the State of Nature enjoys the Executive power of the Law of Nature and therefore '*every Man hath a Right to punish the Offender, and be Executioner of the Law of Nature*' (§ 8).

It is only through enjoying this Executive power of the Law of Nature that any man in the natural condition can come to exercise power over another person given their natural equality and the duty to preserve men in the State or Nature. Because everybody in the State of Nature enjoys fundamental equality and rights under the Law of Nature they cannot be harmed and must be preserved. However, Locke goes on to argue that when someone does harm or kill another, they put themselves beyond the Law of Nature and become an outlaw. They live outside the Law of Nature and by another law. We can therefore regard those who breach the Law of Nature as akin to a '*Lyon* or a *Tyger*, one of those wild Savage Beasts, with whom Men can have no Society'.

What we can see from this argument is that there is violence and force in the State of Nature, but this is only allowed under the guise of punishment, otherwise it is ruled out by the prior obligation to preserve both ourselves and others. The Executive power of the Law of Nature gives rise to two specific rights of punishment. In the first case there is a right to punish based on the idea of restraint. This right to restrain is exercised by all people and not merely those who suffer injury or attack at the hands of criminals and outlaws. The right to restrain can include the imposition of the death penalty on those who threaten murder or who kill. It is in this case that Locke introduces the analogy with the lions, tigers and wild beasts with whom one cannot have society. As these people harm not only their victims but all mankind, all mankind has the duty to restrain their threat and danger.

Locke particularly singles out death as the appropriate punishment for murder. The defence of killing someone as an appropriate punishment, rather than as a mere side effect of defending oneself and others, is not developed to a great extent, but it is clear from the reference to scripture that Locke's argument depends upon an idea of forfeiture, where acting contrary to someone's rights entails in turn the loss of the offender's rights. But does the death penalty apply only to murder? Locke seems to depart from the strict proportionality of 'an eye for an eye'. He argues that in the case of the lesser breaches of the Law of Nature deciding the appropriate punishment will involve judgements of degree and severity sufficient to make the act 'an ill bargain'. This suggests that part of the task of punishment is retributive and part deterrent. The retributive argument supports the necessity and duty of punishing a breach of the law. In such a case we have a duty and not merely a prudential reason to deter some inconvenient actions, for on a strict deterrence theory we might weigh up the cost of punishing against other costs and decide in some cases to withhold punishment because there will be no deterrent effect. For those in the natural law tradition such as Locke, punishment is a duty that falls on us all because of the Law of Nature. We would therefore be doing a wrong by refusing to punish a breach of the Law of Nature. However, deterrent effect does play a role in deciding the severity and nature of the punishment. There is no simple connection between the nature of the crime and the character of the punishment of the sort we might infer from the use of the death penalty to punish murder. It is therefore perfectly possible that the death penalty would be the appropriate deterrent for crimes against property.

As well as the right to restrain breaches of the Law of Nature through punishment, Locke also identifies a further right to reparation. This right is different to the right of restraint as it may only be exercised by the victim of the crime and not by third parties, as is the case with restraint. The right to reparation allows the victim or injured party to recover what is his, either by taking back what was stolen or by recovering the value of what was stolen. This right is clearly designed to prevent anyone else from illegitimately benefiting from the proceeds of crime, but it is also important for Locke's later account of the competence of the political magistrate, for he goes on to claim that only the injured party can decide whether or not to pursue recovery and no one else can claim to 'recover' what was illegitimately gained unless it was theirs in the first instance. If the state or third parties sought to recover the proceeds of crime without returning the full value to the original owners, then they too would be guilty of benefiting from the proceeds of crime that would put them in breach of the Law of Nature.

Locke acknowledges that the idea of a natural right to punish might seem a curious and dangerous doctrine. However, he argues that it is essential to make sense of the idea of the state's right to punish aliens. What gives a king or state the right to punish an alien for a breach of the law of a particular state? It cannot simply be that the king has the power to do so, nor can it be that the alien falls under the king's jurisdiction as that might be precisely the point at issue. Instead it can only be that there is a universal jurisdiction based on the Law of Nature which all can enforce and punish breaches of, irrespective of consent or membership.

Finally, the Executive power of the Law of Nature plays an important part in Locke's account of the origin of political power and authority. For it is precisely the problem of the absence of an impartial judge in cases of executing the Law of Nature that is resolved by establishing a civil authority. We will examine precisely how and why we go about creating such an authority later, but it is clear that Locke thinks the right and authority is also a source of inconvenience and conflict as individuals tend to be partial to their own cases and rather less interested in the harm done to others, especially when this requires pursuit. What we have in Locke's State of Nature is a situation akin to that of the Wild West in Western movies. There is indeed a law and it is enforced, but it is enforced partially and with some judgements collapsing into revenge and vendetta. After all, if a party exceeds what is legitimate as punishment or punishes disproportionately by recovering more than they legitimately have a claim to, they will in turn be in breach of the Law of Nature. This has the effect of triggering a spiral of conflict and dispute. This absence of public and impartial execution of the law is one of the main 'Inconveniences of the State of Nature' (§ 13).

Natural Rights

The final building block of Locke's argument that we are introduced to in the State of Nature is the idea of Natural Rights. This is an important and complex notion and one that Locke does not fully explain. In § 7, where Locke introduces the defence of punishment, he refers to the restraint 'from invading others Rights'. Furthermore, throughout the discussion of punishment he refers to the 'Right' to punish. Yet most of the discussion of the State of Nature focuses on the Law of Nature and its implication that people should be preserved from harm to their 'Life, Health, Liberty or Possessions'. Consequently there are a number of things we need to explain. What does Locke mean by rights? What is added to the concept by calling them 'Natural' rights? How do these rights relate to duties? What rights do we have, according to Locke? How individualistic does the appeal to Natural Rights? make Locke's argument?

The Law of Nature is the source of Locke's theory of Natural Rights. It commands that we preserve ourselves and as far as possible preserve others as our equals. From this law we can derive the idea of basic or fundamental rights. The Law of Nature is the fundamental source of moral or normative claims in Locke's theory, but the real work is done by the rights that are inferred from that law. As the argument develops, the role of Natural Rights in Locke's *Second Treatise* becomes more and more important. Yet the notion of rights that is inferred from the Law of Nature is complex in that Locke gives particular rights different normative dimensions. It is customary to follow Hohfeld's fourfold distinction of the rights into claims, liberties, powers and immunities.[9] At least three of these dimensions are present in Locke's use of the concept. If we begin with the concept of claims, we can see that the appeal to a right involves a normative claim that others have a duty to respect. The right to life is such a claim, in that it imposes a strict duty on others that they refrain from acting in ways that might kill me. The right to life is also a general claim in that it applies to everyone equally and is claimed on behalf of everyone. Claims or claim rights are one of the most basic and familiar conceptions of rights that are found in the history of Natural Law. Liberties on the other hand are more recent additions to the history of natural law. Hobbes uses the idea of a liberty right in his account of the State of Nature, Locke uses it as well but it is not the only dimension of his account of Natural Rights and nor is it the most fundamental. A liberty is the power to do or acquire something in the absence of a prior duty. To have a liberty in this sense is not to have a duty or obligation to do something. This idea is important in Locke's account of the Natural Right to acquire property from the common stock, or in that which was previously un-owned. One has a liberty to acquire that which is un-owned in a way that one does not have a liberty to acquire property in that which is already owned, unless the owner is prepared to sell. The scope of rights as liberties is settled by the existence of other duties and claims. The final dimension I want to draw attention to is the idea of a power and this can also be seen in the case of the rights to property. The idea of a power is the discretionary exercise of a right to vary the rights and duties of others. This is most clearly manifest in the case of actions that establish private property. In such cases an agent is at liberty to acquire what is previously un-owned, but in so acting the agent places subsequent limits on what others can legitimately acquire, consequently the power restricts and transforms the rights and liberties of other agents. The right to acquire property is not only a liberty to take what is un-owned but also a power to legitimately restrict the liberty of others and to impose duties upon them. Different Natural Rights will combine these different dimensions in different ways.

Alongside the three dimensions of rights we can also (following A. John Simmons) identity three different classes of Natural Rights in Locke's argument.[10] We have already seen the first in the idea of general rights, such as the right to life, which all equally hold. But we can also distinguish another kind, namely special rights. Special rights are rights that arise out of special transactions or relations between individuals. This class of special rights can in turn be divided into consensual rights and non-consensual rights, which are clearly present in Locke's argument. Here the idea is quite simple. Non-consensual special rights arise out of an unchosen relationship between people and do not depend upon their consent. Among such rights are those of a parent over a child, the right of an individual to acquire property and the right to punish. Consensual special rights are those rights which arise out of an agreement with other individuals, among which we might include promissory or contractual rights, as well as political rights. This latter class involves the conferment of a power on a particular person or persons by others. So much for the essential features and classes of Natural Rights. But what exactly makes a right a Natural Right?

One obvious feature of Natural Rights is that they occur in the State of Nature prior to the institution of political power and authority. So we can argue that Natural Rights are natural in being pre-political or prior to some institutionalized jurisdiction. In this way we can distinguish Natural Rights from positive rights, or those rights which follow from the authoritative commands of a municipal legislature. Political institutions, legislatures and courts can make or declare rights. Even when these rights are consistent with the Law of Nature their authority is partly explained by their pedigree or source. In the case of Natural Rights, Locke wants to assert that some rights are prior to any set of institutions. Similarly, Locke wishes to distinguish them from conventional rights. One might argue that many of the rights we call moral rights grew up as conventional practices, as we can see from comparing our own moral experience with that of other moral cultures. Locke was particularly interested in cultural variation and what that said about the nature and authority of morality. Equally, he was convinced that there was a basic content to morality that did not vary from place to place, and this is captured in his defence of Natural Rights as being prior to moral and cultural conventions. Given all of this, Locke's argument is that if we strip away the political, legal and social institutions of society we would still have some moral claims that we wish to assert as rights.

There is also another dimension to Locke's description of these rights as natural which relates them to our human natures; consequently we enjoy many of our Natural Rights simply in virtue of our sharing the same natures. We saw in the case of Locke's account of fundamental equality that it is in virtue of our sharing a common rational nature that we fall within the group that deserves the equal concern and respect accorded by rights. This common nature is not shared by those outside it, so for Locke the higher sentient mammals do not enjoy rights (as some modern thinkers claim they do), whatever else we might think about their treatment. At the heart of Locke's account of Natural Rights is a set of what we might now call Human Rights, which we enjoy simply in virtue of our common natures. Among these Natural or Human Rights are the right to life and the right to liberty. However, not all of our Natural Rights follow directly from our common humanity, for as we have seen Locke concedes that there are some special rights we enjoy, even prior to political society, only in virtue of special relationships or as a result of the consent of others. These rights flow indirectly from powers that we enjoy as part of our natures, but they do not hold for all humans equally. Although only humans can become parents, not all humans can exercise the special rights of parents as not all humans are parents. Women do have Natural Human Rights, but not necessarily natural special rights, and as we shall see Locke argues that children do not have natural human rights, although they have the capacity to acquire them in due course. Similarly, only humans can enter into contracts and make promises, but only the particular human agents that enter into a contract or agreement will enjoy the natural special rights that follow from them. Locke's conception of Natural Rights is therefore clearly intended to be broader than simply the set of Human Rights, unless this concept is extended to cover all rights claims. Much of the contemporary literature on Human Rights is concerned with the dangers of extending the category to cover all basic rights claims as opposed to a narrow but fundamental set that apply to all humans wherever they happen to be. It is often argued that the concept of Human Rights should be reserved for the right to life, basic freedom and protection from harms such as torture, yet we often find claims for a Human Right to paid holidays or a particular standard of education and healthcare. Locke's account of Natural Rights is similarly broad in encompassing rights that we have through simply being human and rights that we have through exercising certain human capacities or occupying certain human roles and relationships. Yet Locke's conception of Natural Rights is perhaps more helpful than the modern discourse of Human Rights, as it refers to two dimensions of basic rights, namely that they are not the product of political, legal and social conventions and that they are held in virtue of our common natures. Many contemporary philosophers argue that we use the idea of our human natures as the criterion of moral significance, but also claim that something can only be a right when it is sanctioned within a municipal legal jurisdiction, otherwise it remains merely a claim that there should be a right. Locke's theory is significantly different from such modern theories in that he is not merely asserting a reason for there to be a right, but instead, as with his account of Natural Law, he is claiming that the rights we enjoy in the State of Nature are full and complete Natural Rights and not merely reasons. This brings us to the third question concerning Locke's conception of Natural Rights.

Many scholars have claimed that Locke does not really attach priority to the idea of Natural Rights because of the way they are derived from Natural Law. Indeed some commentators, such as John Dunn, Richard Ashcraft and James Tully, have gone so far as to suggest that Locke's theory is really a theory of natural duties, with rights being only a secondary concept.[11] On this view we are subject to a Law of Nature that each must be preserved, which follows from our being God's workmanship. This law distributes duties on each one of us not to interfere with the self-preservation of others by harming them or depriving them of the means of subsistence, and it is in virtue of these duties that we can infer a Natural Right. Because person x has a duty not to interfere with the self-preservation of person y, person y can be said to hold a right against person x. This gives duty priority and makes the right a derivative concept. Is this the correct interpretation of Locke's argument? I think not, on grounds similar to those advanced by A. John Simmons. Locke does connect the concept of right with the concept of a duty in the case of a special set of rights where strict performance of our duties is indeed required by the Law of Nature. In the case of the right to life we can see that the strict duty to preserve ourselves and others fully specifies the right. In this case there is no discretion as for Locke, unlike modern libertarians such as Nozick, there is no right to suicide. Yet not all of our rights take this form. Some Natural Rights are liberties, such as the right to acquire private property, whereby an agent x is not under a duty to do or refrain from anything. Of course the concept of a duty does play a role in liberty rights through its absence, but this suggests that not all Natural Rights can be reduced to a set of prior duties. Furthermore in the case of powers, such as the power to vary or restrict the rights of others through acquiring property that cannot then be acquired by others, we can see that it is often the Natural Right that specifies the distribution and scope of duties. So although the concepts of right and duty are intimately connected in Locke's argument, he does not claim that the nature of rights is exhaustively translatable into the concept of a duty or that the concept of duty has logical priority. Instead, Locke's argument suggests that in most cases beyond a narrow set of rights, the concept is used to indicate discretion and liberty within the wide sphere of action set by the duties we owe to others. How we exercise the liberty and discretion is a matter of right, in that it is not required by any external authority or set of duties. This function of rights is what makes Locke a liberal rather than a perfectionist. A perfectionist is a philosopher (such as Aristotle) who claims that we have a duty to exercise and cultivate our particularly human capacities in a certain way and that the political community can compel us to act in that way. Locke's argument places constraints upon how far political authority can be exercised over us without our consent, even in order to do us good. Locke's argument does not necessarily result in the kind of liberal position we find in J. S. Mill in the nineteenth century or John Rawls in the twentieth, but it is a mistake to use the concept of duty to turn Locke into a kind of communitarian or to suggest that the concept has logical priority and to play down the important role of individual Natural Rights.

Another criticism of Locke's conception of Natural Rights, which we should note in passing, is advanced by Leo Strauss and Richard Cox, among others.[12] These commentators take the opposite position to Ashcraft and Tully and claim that Locke does indeed attach priority to the concept of Natural Rights but he does so in a way which undermines his claim to be a Natural Law theorist and which entails a corrosive and atomistic individualism. This criticism is part of a broader attack on contemporary liberal modernity for which Locke is an important source. The argument is that the priority of Natural Rights, in particular the Natural Right to self-preservation, entails that Locke's theory is narrowly egoistic and individualistic. Rights are seen to establish barriers between people that society cannot cross and this undermines the idea of a moral community whereby people have obligations and duties as well as rights. This idea of rights-based atomism is certainly reflected in the ideas of contemporary libertarians such as Robert Nozick. The question, of course, is whether this is indeed Locke's view.

We already have seen enough of Locke's argument about the State of Nature to see that this criticism of egoism and atomism is exaggerated. We do indeed have a strict duty to preserve ourselves, but Locke is clear to point out that the injunction to self-preservation grounds an equal right to all people. The Law of Nature therefore moderates the extreme egoism of an unrestricted right to self-preservation of the sort one could find in Hobbes' argument. We cannot, for Locke, preserve ourselves at the expense of others – we cannot kill them except in self-defence or punishment, and we cannot take their property. Our Natural Rights entail duties, although they are not reducible to duties. Secondly, we need to be careful about the charge of atomism. Locke is certainly an individualist and he is unapologetic about that. Some of this individualism is no doubt explainable in terms of Locke's Protestant worldview, but it is not simply reducible to that. Locke does not deny that we have obligations to others, and he does not argue that only rights matter. What he does assert is that rights place limits on the exercise of political, social and legal power, and while these might challenge some claims to authority or conceptions of society, simply to appeal to these traditional conceptions of society and authority in criticism of Locke's argument is a non sequitur as it is precisely the nature and limits of social and political power that he is trying to explain and justify.

The final question concerning Natural Rights is what rights do we have? This is a question with no simple answer. Although Locke is traditionally depicted as defending a right to life, liberty and property, this is too simplistic. He does not provide a full list of rights, but does indicate that there is a diverse range of rights that are not reducible to life, liberty and property. We have already seen for example the two rights of punishment, the right to restrain and the right to recover. The first is a general right applying to all, whereas the second is a special right as it applies only to the victim. Also as Locke distinguishes the idea of liberty under the Law of Nature from licence we can see space for a set of liberties to do certain things instead of a single right to non-interference. In respect of property the right can also be broken down into a series of specific rights to acquire, exchange and consume articles of property. The key point is that Natural Rights are derived from the Law of Nature and we need to explain precisely how rights claims follow from the broad principle of the Law of Nature as a law of preservation. We can see the Rights of Nature as distinct subordinate principles that follow from the broad general principle of the Law of Nature. Natural Rights give specific content to the idea of the Law of Nature, and therefore the full list of Natural Rights is context dependent, in the sense that they follow from the extension of the Law of Nature to new circumstances of human action. On the other hand, Locke clearly does not think that this makes the concept of a Natural Right an indeterminate one, as a Natural Right must be a clear implication of the Law of Nature.

Similarly it would be wrong to consider all of the rights Locke mentions as negative rights involving merely duties of forbearance on the part of others. We might distinguish positive and negative rights on the grounds that positive rights require people to do or provide particular things, whereas negative rights merely require forbearance from acting. In this way, to have a negative right to life, a person merely enjoys the forbearance of others from killing him; it does not entail that others must do anything to help him stay alive, such as provide food or medicine. Strauss and Cox, as we saw, claimed that Locke thought of our Natural Rights in a purely negative or egoistic sense, yet this is clearly not Locke's intention. We do indeed have claims on others in virtue of our Natural Rights in that we can claim that they punish violations of those rights. More controversially, Locke also thinks that in certain (admittedly very dire) circumstances we do have a claim on assistance. This does not make Locke a proto-defender of the welfare state (as he most definitely was not) as he can claim that adequate assistance to preserve ourselves follows from the ability to sell our labour and acquire wages to buy food and shelter, but it does suggest that Locke avoids falling on the negative side of a distinction between positive and negative rights. As Locke's conception of rights entails a claim on others to respect the right holder in certain respects it does not make sense to merely emphasize the idea of forbearance.

State of Nature, history and realism

Locke's State of Nature is an abstract model of life in the absence of political society, and all of the features that we have explored are supposed to explain why we have political power and authority and why it has the character it does. As we shall see in the next sections Locke proceeds to draw some very specific implications from his abstract model of the State of Nature. Yet before turning to draw those implications he offers a brief but important response to one of the residual sceptical arguments against his whole procedure. As we have seen Locke is less concerned about those challenges that argue that we have no evidence for when such a world existed. The historical challenge assumes that Locke thinks the State of Nature existed at a time long ago in the past and challenges it by offering an alternative account of the 'Garden of Eden' or some other original history. In §15 Locke returns to a quote from Hooker and argues that the State of Nature did not occur in the past but is actually occurring in every historical period where men have not consented to put themselves under political rule. So as well as arguing that the State of Nature is an analytical construction, Locke also wants to assert its realism as an account of the world we may find ourselves in. It is for the reader then to decide whether his obligation to the current political order is based on consent and whether the claims of political authority fall within those of the Law of Nature. Locke suggests that the real issue facing State of Nature arguments and his style of rational political philosophy is not the specific challenge from history but the issue of realism or how well they model aspects of actual experience. The passage from Hooker suggests that the State of Nature argument tells us a lot about our actual experience once we understand the point of the argument as justifying political obligation and the boundaries of legitimate political authority rather than explaining the causal origins of particular institutions and conventions.

Yet Locke does not simply want to argue that the State of Nature is a normative model and therefore that it is concerned with normative realism and as such immune to historical claims that there never was such a state of affairs. In the previous section he argues that if we turn away from domestic political affairs and look instead at the relations between states and kingdoms we can see something like the State of Nature as a genuine description of international relations. 'That since all *Princes* and Rulers of *Independent* Governments all over the World, are in a State of Nature, 'tis plain the World never was, nor ever will be, without Numbers of Men in that State' (§ 14).

Again Locke's point is complex, but is supposed to be supported by actual experience and our understanding of it. First, he is claiming that between states or rulers of states there is no higher human legislative institution – there is no world state – but that does not mean that there is no law between rulers. States and their rulers are not entitled to do anything they wish one with another. When one state breaks this natural law another has a right to go to war to punish the breach of the Law of Nature. Secondly, Locke is claiming that it is only in virtue of this law-governed State of Nature that a ruler can punish a non-national for breach of the law. But it is also in virtue of this fact that an alien can seek redress for breach of the law in respect to his property rights, etc. A non-national engaged in international commerce and trade is perfectly entitled to seek punishment for interference with his property or person, even though he has not consented to be ruled by the monarch. Keeping faith or keeping contracts is something that we are obliged to do independently of being members of the same political society. If we did not believe that there was some law underlying our actions in the absence of either political society or an international state we would have little reason to engage in international trade and commerce.

What is also interesting for later theorists of international relations in the twentieth century is Locke's claim that his conception of a State of Nature as a form of society without political authority is a more realistic picture than the idea of a State of Nature as a war of all against all. Modern 'realist' international relations theorists and practitioners claim that is the default position and peace is something that breaks out only intermittently. Consequently, rulers must be prepared for war and should pursue and protect their interests from the threat of others. This view sees international relations as a clash of interests with no higher law to discriminate between legitimate and illegitimate interests. For Locke, such a view would be a world of licence and disorder and as such it would not be a realistic description of actual international relations. Consequently, he offers the kind of criticism often raised against contemporary realist theories of international relations, namely that they are unrealistic and based on particular false theories. Far from being a world of unlimited conflict and war between everyone, international relations is an incomplete society with the absence of a single judge or lawgiver. An interesting question which Locke does not address in the *Second Treatise*, and which we will have to leave unanswered, is whether the inconveniences of the international State of Nature lead rulers to seek an international political society with an international sovereign or state.

THE STATE OF WAR AND SLAVERY

We have spent a long time discussing Locke's account of the State of Nature in Chapter II of the *Second Treatise* because it is in this chapter that he introduces most of the building blocks of his subsequent argument and his direct response to Filmer and indirect response to Hobbesian absolutism. But we are not quite finished with the State of Nature or the original position from which Locke constructs his account of the nature and legitimacy of political power and authority. In the two subsequent chapters on the 'State of War' and 'Slavery' Locke returns to issues that further clarify his conception of the State of Nature and man's fundamental rights and duties.

War

Chapter III, 'Of the State of War' might seem an odd way of continuing the argument, but it is important for it draws an important contrast with the argument of Thomas Hobbes who had described the State of Nature as a state of war of 'all against all'. In Hobbes' case war is the absence of law and sovereign authority. But Locke is also referring back to an older tradition of Natural Law and its ideas of just war that we can find in such thinkers as Thomas Aquinas. Locke and Aquinas are both Natural Law thinkers, although Locke's theory differs significantly from Aquinas' in key respects. What connects them is that both need to explain the idea of war within a conception of a moral law-governed universe. War as a phenomenon must be incorporated into the idea of a world that is structured by the Law of Nature, which as we have seen is a fundamental feature of man's natural condition. It cannot therefore be explained, as it is for Hobbes, merely as the absence of law and sovereign power. Indeed it is important for Locke that the State of War is not simply something that exists outside of political authority, for as we shall see at the end of the *Second Treatise* Locke wants to draw some radical conclusions about what should happen when a monarch or ruler is effectively at war with his own people.

In § 16 Locke defines the State of War as a state of enmity and destruction that arises when a person declares by 'Word or Action' a 'sedate and settled Design' on another person's life. When this design is declared or made manifest the person so threatened has the right to destroy that which threatens his own destruction on the grounds that the Law of Nature requires that all may be preserved. When a person threatens the life of another he effectively forfeits his own right to be preserved and can therefore be killed as one would kill a wild animal or other creature beyond the law. The argument here is similar to the defence of punishment where the infliction of violence and death is justified on the grounds of forfeiture. In § 18 Locke argues that one may kill a thief because, although the thief may not directly threaten my life, in putting himself beyond the Law of Nature and attempting to put me under his power in restricting my freedom or depriving me of my property, I am entitled to assume that he might take away everything else, including my life. As there can be no reparation if the thief does kill me, I do not have to wait for the act and then seek to punish the culprit. My duty of self-preservation entitles me to kill the thief as an unjust aggressor who is effectively waging war with me. The difference in this case is that the breach of the law is a threat or settled design, not an act which having been committed calls for reparation.

Three important features of the argument are already apparent. First, the State of War is not necessarily a passionate and hasty act such as wantonly striking another; instead it is seen as a sedate and settled design on the life of another. Secondly, a threat to the life of another is legitimate grounds for a person or people to assert their right of self-preservation against the potential aggressor. The aggressor must show or declare his intention to threaten the lives of others, but he need not yet have acted on that declared intention in order to be a legitimate target of defence against aggression. Thirdly, Locke has said nothing about a State of War only being possible between rightly constituted authorities such as kings or states. In this way he departs from traditional Just War theory as found in Augustine or Aquinas which asserts that only princes can go to war with one another. For Locke, a State of War can exist between princes, between princes and subjects, and between individuals.

Locke develops the argument further in § 17 when he clarifies the role of the threat or settled intention. Here Locke's argument is that anyone who seeks to put another under his absolute power is effectively declaring war on that person as it involves a declaration of a design on a person's life. The threat to life, according to Locke, can be inferred from the threat to freedom. If a person seeks to enslave another or deprive them of their freedom by subjecting them to absolute power, then Locke argues we may legitimately infer that they also threaten that person's life, as we have no good reason to assume that anyone prepared to take away one's freedom would not also be prepared to take away everything else. This holds true in both the State of Nature and within the state of political society.

We are now in a position to see how Locke's argument is an answer to the conflation of the State of Nature and the State of War that is to be found in Hobbes. In § 19 Locke denies that the State of Nature is a world of 'Malice, Violence and Mutual Destruction'. Instead it is properly understood as a state in which men live without a common superior on earth with the power to judge between them. This might well be a world in which there is conflict, but it is not such a world by definition. Indeed Locke goes on to argue that it is the absence of a common judge to appeal to that gives a person a right to go to war against another. This right can indeed be exercised by individuals even in a civil society where there is a legitimate authority, if that authority is unable to preserve a person. So in the event of burglary an individual householder retains the right to go to war against a thief even if there is a public authority, if that authority cannot be appealed to quickly enough in such an emergency. In this case the victim and the aggressor are effectively in a State of Nature without a common power. Consequently, we must see a State of Nature as the absence of a common power or authority to judge between individuals, whereas a State of War is initiated when one uses 'Force without Right' to threaten a man. The State of Nature can be a State of War but is not necessarily one; similarly and importantly for Locke, the State of War can obtain within a society or state if its functionaries and rulers use force without right or legitimacy. Locke is quite explicit about this in § 20 where he writes:

> . . . where an appeal to the Law, and constituted Judge lies open, but the remedy is deny'd by a manifest perverting of Justice, and a barefaced wresting of the Laws, to protect or indemnifie the violence or injuries of some Men, or Party of Men, *there* it *is* hard to imagine any thing but a *State of War*. For wherever violence is used, and injury done, though by hands appointed to administer Justice, it is still violence and injury . . .

Although the creation of an authoritative judge can take us out of a State of Nature with the threat of a State of War, Locke does not go as far as Hobbes in arguing that the creation of a political society ends the possibility of a State of War. Rulers and individuals within a society can then put us into a State of War in which one can legitimately exercise the right of war as a right of self-preservation. Locke returns to the problem this claim raises in the final chapters of the *Second Treatise*.

Slavery

Chapter IV, on Slavery, addresses a different set of questions that arise from the account of the State of Nature and State of War. The discussion of slavery in Locke's *Second Treatise* is a controversial matter for a number of reasons, not least that while in the employment of the Earl of Shaftesbury, Locke was involved in the drafting of the Fundamental Constitution of Carolina which allowed that every freeman 'shall have absolute power and authority over his negro slaves'. It is also important because the premise of fundamental equality which underlies his Law of Nature would seem to rule out the idea of slavery altogether. To be placed under the absolute power of another man is contrary to the Law of Nature and as we have just seen an appropriate ground for the right of war. How is slavery possible in Locke's theory and does he really endorse the holding of slaves as property?

Locke clearly rejects one possible argument for slavery, namely that derived from Aristotle's *Politics* which claims that there is a certain class of people who are natural slaves because of the lack of capacity to be free men. As we saw in Locke's defence of equality the criterion of freedom is best conceived as a range-property which people can exercise with more or less skill and success so that there will be very few if any recognizable human beings who could be considered natural slaves because of lack of reason. Maybe very young children would fall into this class as well as the elderly and mentally infirm, but these are not generally the sole class of people anyone would want to enslave.

A second argument might be that slaves have consented to their enslavement. In § 22 Locke reiterates his argument that a person can be under no legitimate power on earth that she has not consented to. This might seem to leave open the possibility of consenting to enslavement or the slave contract. Many contemporary libertarians, such as Robert Nozick, do leave open the possibility of consenting to enslavement.[13] For Nozick we are able to consent to putting ourselves under the authority of another, including consenting to that person deciding the limits of our freedom and our right to life. Indeed if we were not able to do this we would not be able to consent to submit ourselves to political authority with the right to impose punishment up to and including the death penalty. According to Nozick we are self-owners and therefore can subject what we own to the direction of another, the important point is only that we must consent to our initial enslavement. Nozick's argument has proved to be hugely controversial, but it differs significantly from that of Locke.

For Locke, we are not strictly self-owners, as we are the ultimate property and possession of our creator. At best for Locke, we can be described as having a conditional leasehold in ourselves. Consequently, Locke argues against the concept of negative freedom found in Filmer, claiming that natural freedom is constrained by the Law of Nature which gives us both rights and duties to preserve ourselves. As we have a duty to preserve ourselves we cannot place ourselves under the arbitrary rule of another who might kill us if he saw fit. The arbitrary rule of a slave owner includes the right to destroy his property and potentially to kill his slaves. But why can't he just transfer that discretion? Locke's point clarifies another dimension of his theory of Natural Rights, namely that our most fundamental rights are inalienable. What this means is that we can under no circumstances give these rights up to another person to dispose of as they see fit. We can no more alienate our fundamental right to life to a ruler any more than to a slave owner. Even the rightful judge of a political society can only kill a person as punishment for a breach of the fundamental Law of Nature. He cannot kill a person because it is convenient to do so or because the victim is a political inconvenience. The Law of Nature applies always and everywhere and it establishes fundamental rights that individuals are not entitled to alienate or waive. Consequently, Locke could never condone a right to suicide as a natural or basic moral right.

Yet if it is the case that there are no natural slaves and that we cannot enter into a slave contract, that would seem to settle the issue and leave no room for the idea of slavery in Locke's argument. But in §§ 23–4 Locke does advance another argument that is consistent with his claim for natural liberty under the Law of Nature; it also seems to have been his attempt to explain the right of holding black slaves in the Carolina colonies. His argument returns to his theory of the Right of War.

By entering into a State of War and threatening the life and liberty of another, an individual puts himself outside the protection of the Law of Nature and others can claim the Right of War, which is the right to kill the aggressor. However, if the aggressor is captured, then the captor does have a right to enslave the captive. Locke's argument in § 23 is that enslavement is merely the deferral of the death penalty on one who has already forfeited his right to life. As that right to life becomes forfeit in threatening war, the captive continues to be outside the Law of Nature and therefore no longer the beneficiary of Natural Rights. In effect Locke argues that the State of War continues between the conqueror and his captive and it is only for this reason that the captive can continue in slavery. It is important to add that consent by the captive forms no part of the arrangement as 'No body can give more Power than he has himself: and he that cannot take away his own Life, cannot give another power over it . . .' (§ 23). The right to defer the execution of the Right of War remains the exclusive concern of the conqueror, and this Right of War only obtains if the captive has been engaged in illegitimate force and war.

Locke does seem to have thought that black African slaves at work in the American colonies were captives who had forfeited their right to life. But even if this were the case it raises a number of problems of which Locke was aware. The right to defer the execution of a captive and thus enslave him, if it exists at all, can only apply to the captive and not to his family and dependants. The enslavement of black females who were not engaged in war or the threat of war would be illegitimate and indeed grounds for war against the slave catchers. A similar argument applies to children. Furthermore, the right of ownership would also only extend over one generation. One could not be born into slavery as the result of slave parents. If Locke were to allow this then he would be making a concession to Filmer-type arguments for absolutism, as a conqueror could then gain a right to rule in perpetuity over a people because he had defeated them in war. On such a view the descendants of William the Conqueror would have a claim to absolute power over subsequent generations of Englishmen. Clearly Locke would object to such an argument as inconsistent with natural freedom and equality. Furthermore, the right to enslave as a deferral of the right to kill an aggressor does not for Locke establish a title to that person's property. One could restore what has been stolen to a rightful owner, but taking what legitimately belongs to a person captured in war is not permissible and it establishes no right to real or moveable property. Finally, Locke's argument does not necessarily entail a right to trade slaves captured in battle. It is not obvious that because European slave traders bought black African slaves from African slavers that that fact establishes a legitimate right in the European slave traders.

Locke does not give us a clear answer to these questions but we need to be careful how we interpret that silence and his practical involvement in the regulation and justification of black African slavery in the American colonies. This is clearly a highly emotional issue and rightly so, as the unspeakable practices of black slavery runs contrary to every liberal egalitarian value that Locke seems committed to. Yet one might also read Locke's philosophical argument as a highly qualified right to enslave that would have put the practice of slavery in the American colonies out of business very quickly. Locke's argument, like Aristotle's according to some commentators, raises the bar of justification so high that the institutional practice of it in Locke's day could never actually be justified. Maybe, given the weight of biographical evidence, this interpretation is too generous to Locke on this issue, but whether that is so or not, it is clear that the argument as he presents it does not provide the kind of justification that would have supported the subsequent development of the practice in the Americas. Nor, most importantly, would it provide any basis for a racial conception of slavery. If Locke does indeed justify enslavement he does so in a way that allows for white slaves as well as black.

iii PRIVATE PROPERTY

Although Locke seems to have been particularly proud of the discussion of private property, referring obliquely in his correspondence to the *Second Treatise* as one of the best discussions of property, and although the discussion of the concept has become one of the staples of controversy among Locke scholars and subsequent philosophers, some commentators have queried the point of Chapter V in the overall structure of his argument. Lloyd-Thomas, for example, argues that Locke's main concern in the *Second Treatise* is an account of legitimate political rule and political obligation so the appearance of the discussion of private property between the account of the State of Nature and the defence of political obligation and consent is a curiosity.[14] There is something to this claim, yet its force might well follow from a too contemporary understanding of the nature and point of political philosophy. We might on such a view tend to see the only point of political philosophy in normative terms, justifying our obligation to obey the state as we can turn to history and sociology to explain the origins of government. Indeed this seems partly to be Locke's argument, where he draws on history, whether it be scriptural or speculative, to explain how political communities arose, but where he turns to normative philosophical arguments to explain legitimacy and obligation. But even with this similarity of argument there is an important difference between Locke's position and that of contemporary liberal theories. Locke wished to explain the nature and limits of political obligation and legitimate political rule and as we shall see he did this with the idea of consent. Yet political rule cannot exist merely in abstract, but needs to apply to a particular community, or civil society to use Locke's term. The question we need to answer is what is that civil society? One answer which Locke gives in § 96 is that civil or political society is a community of those who have consented to become one body politic under a single government. This is certainly part of Locke's answer but it is potentially incomplete as it says nothing about the limits of jurisdiction of this political society. In other words, the argument from consent seems to presuppose the idea of a territorially concentrated political community over which its jurisdiction is exercised. This is indeed an important part of the idea of the modern state. Yet we need to explain the legitimate nature of this idea of territorial jurisdiction. Contemporary political philosophers tend to regard the issue of jurisdiction as a conventional matter and focus on the issue of legitimacy, on the grounds that most states and political societies emerge as accidents of history and the only important question is how they can be made legitimate in the eyes of their members and those of other states. Locke, however, cannot rely on the idea of convention as that would open the door to some of the claims of political absolutism that he wishes to reject. If territorial jurisdiction is a matter of convention and not consent then it can be changed without consent and a new convention can emerge. This argument would not only effect the boundaries of states or political communities but would also affect the enjoyment of property within the state. If the territorial boundary of a civil society is conventional then so would be the territorial claims of individuals within that state and this would open the door to political authority interfering with property without consent.

Locke's strategy is to reverse the whole direction of this problem by making territorial jurisdiction itself dependent upon pre-political rights to private property and in particular pre-political rights to real property in land. If we already own parts of the world privately, then the pooling of these pieces of individual territory as part of the voluntary consent to become part of a civil society explains the extent of that society's territorial jurisdiction. But it also means that because these rights are prior to civil society they cannot be subject to change or interference within civil society without the consent of the original owner. So we need an account of private property rights in the State of Nature if we are to have an account of territorially concentrated political societies and in this sense it is perfectly clear why Locke thought he needed to address the justification of private property rights before going on to explain the origin of political society in subsequent chapters. Private property rights are an essential component of the kind of individualistic and voluntaristic political associations that Locke wished to defend. This form of argument has also proved immensely attractive to many subsequent political philosophers from Kant to Nozick, who wish to limit the nature and claims of the state to the protection of rights. It also forms an important part of the response to the individualist anarchist, who asks: why do we need any kind of state at all?

In providing an answer to one set of questions concerning the territorial claims of political societies, Locke's individualistic methodology has opened up another set of problems. How, for example, do these pre-political rights to private property arise? As we shall see shortly, Locke provides some ingenious if ultimately unsuccessful arguments in justification of individual rights to private property in the world. But before turning to those arguments we need to examine the context in which Locke developed his individualistic argument.

Once again the central concern underlying Locke's radical approach is to challenge Filmer's patriarchalist account of property rights. At the heart of Filmer's argument is the claim that God had given dominion over the whole world to Adam at the creation. This involved the donation of political power, but it also involved territorial jurisdiction over the whole world. So Filmer's patriarchal theory is not merely an account of political rule as a species of paternal rule, it is also an argument about the origin and nature of property. This was the most attractive part of Filmer's argument to patriarchal absolutists as it meant that the king could tax without consent as he was the heir to Adam and the ultimate owner of all the land in his realm. The territory of any particular state was effectively the personal property of the king and was only enjoyed on an extended lease by his subjects. The important point about Filmer's argument is that it combines an apparently scriptural argument with an argument from convention. The conventional component concerned the particular rules governing property in the king's realm. As the law of property was merely a form of convention concerning the disposition of the king's own property it could indeed be varied without consent. This could lead to taxation without representation and expropriation of property as an arbitrary punishment for disobedience.

While we might find Filmer's main argument for the grant of dominion to Adam rather weak, there was a further aspect to Filmer's position which gave it additional strength and that was his critique of the alternative argument for the origin of private property, namely consent. If the world was not given to Adam as personal property as Filmer claimed, then it must be the common resource of all mankind, a point conceded by Locke who claimed that both reason and revelation indicate that the world was given to mankind in common (§ 25). Even if one is not persuaded by the reference to the book of Psalms (although Locke's reference here is important as it contradicts Filmer's claim that scripture provides univocal support for God's donation of the world to Adam), the Law of Nature as a law of reason shows that the world is a common resource from which we can draw that which we need for our preservation. It would not make sense to have a right and duty to preserve ourselves but be denied access to the material conditions of our sustenance and survival.

But if the world is given to us in common, Filmer asks how can anyone come to have individual property in land and its produce? Certainly we can take and eat what we need, although we would have no right to protest at someone taking food from our hands, but we would certainly not have a right to exclude others. The standard answer which Filmer mocked was that private property was based on consent. This was indeed the argument of Locke's enormously influential (but now relatively neglected) contemporary, the German philosopher Samuel Pufendorf (1632–94). He claimed that the world was given to man as a resource owned in common, and it was only the result of the consent of all others that enabled individuals to take and exclude others from portions of the common property of all mankind. Pufendorf went on to argue that this primitive possession was then pooled during the contractual creation of particular political societies, but he also argued that in creating such societies individuals alienated their primitive property to the sovereign who then in return created publicly recognized property within his realm. Real property rights were therefore a social convention and could be altered by the sovereign who exercised an ultimate power of eminent domain over all the rights of his subjects. This strategy was clearly unattractive to Locke, but the more pressing problem pointed out by Filmer was the difficulty of basing the initial acquisition of private property on the idea of consent.

While Locke was not averse to consent-based arguments, when it came to justifying individual claims to private property, he recognized insurmountable problems. In the first instance the agreement to private takings from the common property of mankind would require all the rest of mankind to give their consent. This could not be given by small groups of people in territorially concentrated areas as Locke argued could be the case with the founding of political societies. The agreement of all mankind was required to justify private takings. If such an agreement had taken place we would certainly have some record of it and clearly even Filmer thought we had no such evidence. But even if such evidence did exist it is not obvious that it would provide a justification for the move from common property to private property as there is always the problem of future generations who would be having their rights altered by an initial agreement that they could not be party to, and therefore could not consent to. If such a one-off agreement could bind all future generations then a similar argument could be made for political authority, whereby an initial agreement by some people in the past could bind the liberty of future generations to a particular political authority irrespective of their consent. Once again the threat of Hobbesian absolutism arose.

If the consent argument does not work because there has been no original agreement to authorize the transition from common to private property, then we are faced with a world in which there are no legitimate rights to private property as everyone holds a veto over any individual's claim to private ownership. This, however, is a bizarre conclusion according to Locke as it would preclude the possibility to taking resources from the common stock to secure our own subsistence and self-preservation and consequently it would appear to be contrary to the Law of Nature (§ 28). We must either then agree with Filmer or some other conventional account of property acquisition, or alternatively find another account of private acquisition that is compatible with the Law of Nature. This is precisely what Locke attempts.

Self-ownership

Locke's highly original and subsequently influential argument starts from the idea that we have an initial private property right in our own person. This has become known as the 'self-ownership' argument. He writes:

... every Man has a *Property* in his own *Person*. This no Body has any Right to but himself. The *Labour* of his Body, and the *Work* of his Hands, we may say, are properly his. Whatsoever then he removes out of the State that Nature hath provided, and left it in, he hath mixed his *Labour* with, and joined to it something that is his own, and thereby makes it his *Property*. (§ 27)

This argument has become very influential in contemporary political philosophy through its restatement in Robert Nozick's *Anarchy, State and Utopia*, and its extensive discussion by philosophers such as G. A. Cohen and Michael Otsuka.[15] Locke's clear assertion is that we have at least one primordial source of individual private property claims and this is located in our person. As we are individuated persons rather than merely aspects of a group, whether culture, race or nation, our most basic property right is a private or individuated one. The clear implication is that individual rights claims enjoy pre-eminence over group or collective rights.

Although it is undoubtedly Locke's argument that we own ourselves, this is a rather surprising claim for him to make given his earlier account of the origin of our Natural Rights. As we have already seen in the account of the State of Nature, Locke argues that we are moral equals who enjoy rights against one another because ultimately we are part of the created order and are therefore the property of God. Because we are already the property of someone else we may not kill ourselves and we have a duty to preserve ourselves and all others like us, where doing so is not incompatible with our self-preservation. Strictly speaking for Locke we are not self-owners in the same way that Nozick or Cohen think we might be self-owners. Both of these contemporary philosophers accept that self-ownership gives us a full property right to our persons such that we can destroy ourselves through self-abuse or suicide, and in Nozick's case we can even alienate our property in ourselves to another, by selling ourselves into slavery. Locke rejects the idea that we can sell ourselves into slavery and argues that if slavery is possible it is only so in virtue of the forfeiture of rights that arises through the pursuit of an unjust aggression. Similarly Locke cannot countenance a right to suicide.

Consequently, we should interpret Locke's argument to entail not a full right to self-ownership, but rather a qualified right, more like that enjoyed by a leaseholder than a freeholder. That said, we should note that Locke is still making an important claim when he argues that we have a property in our person. His point is that although we may be the property of God, continuing to exist at his discretion, we cannot be the property of any power other than God. The claim is rather like that made by republics such as the United States to be one nation 'under God'. The point here is not simply an act of piety, it is also the acknowledgement that a republic cannot be subject to any higher human power or law. Similarly in Locke's case the person cannot be subject to any higher human power unless they have agreed to subject themselves to it. In this way Locke's claim that we own ourselves is another assertion of his fundamental egalitarianism. If we cannot be naturally subject to any higher power and we cannot be owned by any human power, then we are all, at least in this respect, moral equals.

We should also note that Locke's claim is not just that we own our bodies, and therefore that we cannot be used as a tool for the good of others. His claim is that we own our persons, which is a more complex claim. What Locke means by the person is a very complex question as it potentially refers to ideas developed in his *An Essay Concerning Human Understanding* that do not fit well with the claim being advanced here. In that work he draws on the idea of experience and memory along with bodily continuity to explain the idea of the person. Here he is referring to ideas such as labour and the work of one's hands as expressions of the person that we ultimately own. Labour in some highly ambiguous sense of that word seems to be an expression of our persons so that whatever we labour on is connected to our persons or that which we ultimately and exclusively own.

The self-ownership argument is only the first premise of Locke's complex argument but already it raises a number of questions, not least concerning precisely what it means to own oneself. The first question that has been raised by a number of modern critics is whether ownership is indeed the kind of relationship that one can enjoy with one's person or self. If one owns a pair of trousers these can be removed from the person, sold, destroyed or given away. In other words the object of ownership is separable from the person. Yet clearly our relationship with ourselves is not like that at all; indeed it is argued we cannot actually have a relationship with ourselves as this would suggest there is something that the person is relating to, but what would that be other than the person? Perhaps we can have a relationship with ourselves over time, so that a person at t_1 might be said to bind themselves at t_2 by entering into an agreement such as a promise or a contract. This form of self-binding is compatible with Locke's philosophical account of personal identity in the *Essay*, but it is not the kind of relationship that we are supposed to have in regarding our person as property. Even if we were to try and alienate ourselves by consenting to our enslavement, there is an important sense in which we are not giving ourselves away on the analogy with the trousers, as we would be continuous with our self or person and therefore we would not be alienating ourselves at all.

An alternative way of making sense of Locke's claim might be to see the relation as one between aspects of our personality. This interpretation is perhaps supported by the references to labour and the work of our hands. In this case our labour is an expression of ourselves and it is this which we can alienate or give away. But this only moves the ambiguity from the concept of the person to the concept of labour. J. P. Day and Jeremy Waldron provide an analysis of six senses of the concept of labour, each of which fails to fit Locke's claim that we can enjoy a primordial ownership relation with our labour.[16] Three of these senses are derived from uses of the concept that apply to objects separate from the person, such as the products of labour, the collection of labourers as in 'organized labour' or the tasks, jobs or employment of labourers and therefore they need not concern us. That leaves three senses that might apply to the person in the way Locke suggests.

1. Labour as an activity. Here the claim is that we can speak of labour as something that we engage in. But this 'adverbial' sense of labour is inadequate to explain Locke's claim as once we have engaged in the activity the labour ceases or disappears.
2. We might refer to labour power – a sense taken up by Marx and his followers in his labour theory of value. However, this sense of labour is not something that can be transferred to objects in the way Locke seems to suggest. The relevant power seems to remain with the person.
3. Labour in the sense of the force or energy expended in the activity of working.

Although the third sense might be stretched to capture something of Locke's argument, none of these senses really seem to fit his conception of self-ownership as they either cannot be alienated or else they tend to be expended in their exercise, so that there is nothing left to own once one has ceased to labour. This matters when we connect the premise of self-ownership to Locke's major claim for initial acquisition of private property.

Original acquisition

Although we might be said to own ourselves, at least in the minimum sense of not being owned by anyone else, this still leaves the problem of the world being owned in common. Before we turn to how Locke explains individual claims to real property in land we need to return to precisely how we should interpret the right to common property in the world. If the claim that the world is owned by each of us is interpreted in terms of each of us having a common claim-right over the whole world, then it is scarcely possible that anyone could have a private property right in any part of the world as everyone would have a veto over initial acquisition. But that merely raises the question of why we should regard the common right to the world as a claim-right imposing strict duties on all others. Locke's argument challenges this reading of the common right to the world. Instead Locke's claim that reason and revelation show that the world was given to mankind in common suggests not a common property right in the world, but rather a common resource from which each of us is at liberty to draw what we need to secure our self-preservation. So the world is a common resource from which each of us is not under a duty NOT to take what we need. (The double negative of not being under a duty not to do something is what comprises a liberty right.) The world is a common stock from which we are at liberty to draw the means of our self-preservation. If the argument were merely concerned with how we justify taking immediate possession of an un-owned apple for our sustenance, the argument could stop there. However, Locke wanted to justify the acquisition and exclusive taking and enclosure of land (§ 32). To do this he needed more than a right to take immediate temporary possession of the means of subsistence; he needed an additional argument to justify exclusive takings. In fact Locke offered two distinct arguments; the 'labour-mixing' argument (§§ 27–8) and the labour theory of value (§§ 40–6).

The labour-mixing had already been prefigured in Locke's claim that we are self-owners. He had claimed that as we labour on the un-owned matter of the world, we mix something of our own with that matter and in so doing acquire an exclusive claim to it. To deny this claim to exclusive ownership would entail allowing others to claim ownership of part of my person. Consequently, we can see how important the self-ownership argument is for Locke. Without it we do not have anything to mix with the world that we do not merely expend or lose.

Locke's argument is a curious one and difficult to defend, but it does draw on some intuitions we have about work and labour and the transformation of the world. Given that Locke claims this argument supports the acquisition of property in land (§ 32), we might think of the first cultivator of virgin land in a new colony. The colonist clears the land of trees, roots and rocks, and then encloses it from the common stock of nature. This piece of land is then ploughed – literally mixing the sweat of one's brow with the newly cut soil – and then cultivated. A similar sort of physical relationship is established with the process of harvesting. Although the image does not withstand much philosophical scrutiny we can see the intuitive appeal of claiming that the farmer has mixed his labour – the sweat of his brow – with that which has previously been left unused. If someone were to come and interfere with his crops and take his produce we would tend to regard this as unfair and taking advantage of someone. We might also think of this as taking what already belongs to someone else. Yet this is where the argument starts to get difficult. If we test our intuitions, we might certainly think that the farmer has the right to his crops which would not have existed without his labour. In this sense the labour does indeed seem to connect with the property claim. If he grew potatoes, then arguably they would not have existed without his effort and therefore he is not taking them from the common stock. Anyone coming along and helping themselves to his potatoes would not be exercising their right to something that was common. The potatoes were never part of that common stock. In this case we might argue that there is a property claim being established here, although it may not be based on mixing one's labour, as we shall see shortly. But what we have not done is establish a claim to ownership of the land on which the crop is cultivated. Enclosing the land is indeed taking something from the common stock for exclusive use and enjoyment and it is much less clear that the farmer's working of the land gives him a right to exclude others who might consider the land a common resource for traditional hunting, for a general right of way, or merely for walking one's dog. None of these activities involves taking the crop of the farmer; they merely involve challenging the exclusive claim to use the land, and it is not obvious why mixing one's labour with the land creates this exclusive right.

Robert Nozick famously tests the intuition behind this argument with his example of tipping a can of tomato juice into the un-owned ocean.[17] Assume that labour is indeed the kind of thing that can be owned and mixed in the relevant sense, like a can of tomato juice. If we mix that with what was previously un-owned, do we actually acquire ownership of the ocean or do we merely lose our tomato juice? Nozick does not actually say that this test completely undermines Locke's argument, but it does seem a peculiarly problematic claim. After all, when one mixes the tomato juice with the ocean it is presumably possible for the molecules of tomato juice to disperse throughout the whole ocean. Does the same thing happen when we mix our labour with land? Do we acquire only the plot we work upon or does our labour disperse throughout the un-owned territory? If we use the 'sweat of our brow' image then perhaps the same kind of dispersal might indeed take place. If the argument is more confined then we need to know how much more confined. Does our labour merely give us a title to the small plot immediately beneath our fence post and not the whole of the enclosed field? Does it merely include the narrow furrows actually scored in the earth by the plough but not the earth around them? This might all seem like 'nit-picking' but it does draw attention to the fact that the intuitive appeal of Locke's argument is on the surface and that beneath that surface appeal the argument is both unclear and inconclusive.

Although the labour-mixing argument seems unsalvageable, many subsequent thinkers have tried to draw something from it. They have generally conceded the claim about the weakness of basing a claim to ownership of land on the grounds of mixing one's labour and have instead focused on claims to property in the produce of labour. As Locke wanted to base his account of territorial jurisdiction on the pre-political right to private property he cannot concede the terrain so easily. Yet we can also see in Locke's account of the labour theory of value an alternative justification of original acquisition.

Throughout Locke's chapter on property he places considerable emphasis on the importance of labour. Initially labour is part of the personal property with which his argument starts, but for much of the chapter he turns to the transformative potential of labour and the way in which it is labour and work which create most of that which is of value. Indeed in § 40 he even tries to compute the relative contributions of natural resource and labour to the value of property. Without labour we would have none of the benefits of industry, building and culture and this emphasis on labour also explains why European countries were rich while resource-rich territories such as North America were poor and lacking in the development of modern material culture, with the tribal prince of such regions '. . . clad worse than a day Labourer in *England*'. The long praise of labour throughout the chapter should not be overstated, as Locke does not see labour in the way Marx saw it, as the highest good and purpose of man. Labour is work and tiresome, but it also has its rewards and therefore it is, according to Locke, only right that the industrious should be better off than the 'idle and contentious'. Here we can see some of the evidence used by Laski and Macpherson for arguing that Locke is an early advocate of the relationship between a Protestant ethic of hard work and its rewards, and the so-called 'spirit of Capitalism'.[18] Whether this is fair or not, the emphasis on the value-creating aspect of labour provides an alternative defence of initial acquisition.

This argument draws on Locke's claim that the produce of labour is not part of the common stock in the first instance. And as we have just seen Locke goes some way to demonstrating that the input of natural resources is at best a very small component of the value created by labouring. Thus the labourer has a *prima facie* case to own that which he has produced, other things being equal. If we go back to the example of the farmer cultivating potatoes on previously un-cleared ground, we acknowledged the intuitive plausibility of the farmer's claim to his produce, even if there was room to doubt the claim to the land that was enclosed. The intuitive plausibility of this argument is bolstered by the recognition that as the produce would not have existed without the labour, nobody can claim a share of it on the basis of their claim to the common stock. Thus the producer does indeed seem to have a *prima facie* right to the produce. Furthermore, we might claim that it is unfair to deprive the producer of what he has produced so that coercive expropriation would be an unjust act. It is precisely this kind of argument that Robert Nozick uses in his 'Lockean' critique of contemporary theories of distributive justice. Notice that the argument from fairness does not make any reference to mixing something that was previously owned with raw nature. One can gain a title to what one has produced even if we cannot trace any tangible substance called 'labour' within the structure of the object produced. In this sense Locke's argument can indeed draw on the more common 'adverbial' senses of labour as an activity. The downside of this argument from the fair enjoyment of the value produced by labouring is that it does not provide an exclusive claim to real property in land. This might not matter for Locke's successors, but it matters for Locke's argument as he needs to base his account of the territorial jurisdiction of the state on pre-political property holdings in land.

World-ownership and equality

There is one important feature of Locke's account of initial acquisition that we have not considered and that is the egalitarian base-line that is implicit in his argument. At one level Locke does not seem particularly bothered by the issue of distributive equality of land or property as is illustrated by his claim that God gave the world to the industrious. Locke's labour theory has been seen as one of the clearest expressions of the Protestant roots of capitalism with its implication that material inequality is part of the natural order and the appropriate reward for hard work and effort. If Locke does have a theory of distributive justice it must place great emphasis on desert. This is indeed the claim made by libertarians such as Robert Nozick, who use Lockean arguments to support a minimal state with no responsibility for the welfare or material equality of the worst off. Whilst there is much to the claim that Locke was a defender of a minimal state and had (from a modern perspective) particularly harsh views about the treatment of the poor and unemployed, there is another important sense in which he is committed to a strict form of egalitarianism. As we saw at the outset, Locke's theory of Natural Law and Natural Rights involves the recognition of fundamental equality in respect of rights to life and liberty. The right to property is potentially more ambiguous. Clearly Locke believed that on the basis of the Law of Nature each person has a right to acquire the means to their own self-preservation. This entails an equal right to acquire property. However, a right to acquire property is a very different thing to a right to an equal amount of property. When it comes to individual property holdings, Locke believed that these holdings should reflect labour and effort. So the labour theory of acquisition allows for material inequality among equal rights holders. But however great the amount of value created by labour, at some level all labour must use the material resource of nature, which as we saw is a common resource. And however intuitively plausible it is to give the individual labourer the product of his labour, the claim to exclusive ownership of material resources in the world is more controversial. Locke has attempted to explain how this initial acquisition might be done using his two arguments based on labour. Yet the initial takings can only be justified if they do not undermine the equal rights to acquire property that Locke claims all humans possess. He therefore needs a way of showing how initial acquisition is compatible with the common rights of all others, at least to the extent of not making them worse off. This point applies in the case of both the labour-mixing argument and the fairness argument.

Locke recognized this problem by introducing two necessary conditions on the just initial acquisition of property. These are the 'enough and as good' condition (§ 27) and the 'non-spoilage' constraint (§ 31). I will deal with the latter of these conditions first, as it is the most straightforward.

The non-spoilage constraint is a clear implication of the Law of Nature to preserve as much as may be preserved. This is the basic justification for taking from the common stock and therefore it would be somewhat curious if we could take things from nature, not to use but merely to spoil and waste. Locke's abhorrence of waste follows closely from his enthusiasm for labour and creativity. As labour creates value so spoilage destroys it. Consequently, the non-spoilage constraint places limits on what portion of land can be taken and enclosed, as we cannot claim ownership of land so extensive that we cannot cultivate it and turn it to human purposes. But the constraint also applies to the way nature can be used in producing what is not part of the common stock. Locke also agrees that the rightful accumulation of produce from one's own land is constrained by the ability to consume it or trade it. If a farmer is particularly successful and produces more grain than he can ever use without it spoiling, then his just right to property only extends to that portion that he can use. By implication others would have a title to the surplus produce if it was otherwise to spoil and decay. This might seem to open the door to a claim to social distribution, but this would be reading too much into Locke's argument. The constraint applies to individual acquisition in the State of Nature before the invention of money. It limits the right of the producer but does not entail a duty to anyone else. That others have a right to the surplus only follows from the fact that the surplus is not technically private property and therefore remains part of the common stock from which individuals are at liberty to take – also interestingly the claim seems to suggest that labour can be wasted as well as mixed! Locke does not take the problem of overproduction too seriously, as he still sees labour as difficult and demanding such that rational individuals would not needlessly labour to produce without limit just for the sake of it. Furthermore, in the natural condition this sort of overproduction is difficult to achieve and sustain. So even though Locke does acknowledge that we can have a natural or pre-social desire for more than we need (§ 37), he does not think that is strong enough to encourage many men to overproduce. The non-spoilage constraint is therefore fairly easily satisfied in the State of Nature.

More problematic is the first constraint, or the requirement that property may be acquired only '. . . where there is enough, and as good left in common for others' (§ 27). This constraint has attracted considerable attention because it seems on one simple reading to render the just initial acquisition of resources untenable. Indeed many contemporary philosophers, such as G. A. Cohen, have used the interpretation of the 'enough and as good' constraint as the basis for a rejection of the Nozick's 'Lockean' libertarianism and the claim that self-ownership is incompatible with a commitment to egalitarianism.[19] Other famous commentators on Locke, such as C. B. Macpherson, have also argued that the constraint undermines the possibility of an initial right to acquisition as this would always leave others with less from which to make their acquisition and therefore could not be '. . . leaving as much and as good' for others. Given the deep controversy surrounding this constraint and the potential problem it poses for Locke's argument the question for us is how we should interpret the constraint.

Jeremy Waldron has argued that Locke does not actually present the requirement to leave '. . . enough and as good . . .' as a constraint on appropriation – that is as a principled limitation on the acquisition of a right. Instead Waldron argues that what he calls the 'sufficiency' constraint depends upon a forced reading of Locke's argument and that the only genuine constraint derived from the Law of Nature is that of non-spoilage.

The problem with the traditional reading of the '. . . enough and as good . . .' constraint is that it seems to make the initial acquisition of property impossible. Even if we consider that in a hypothetical initial position there are very few people and a very large world, the takings of one person, even though leaving plenty for others to acquire, would always leave the others with less then they could have acquired in the first instance. In consequence we might claim that the condition should be interpreted as an equal share in the resources and territory of the world. Thus we might argue, as long as the initial appropriator does not take more than his fair share the condition is satisfied and the acquisition is legitimate. But even this version is problematic, as how do we measure equal shares of land and resources? At the time Locke was writing, a large share of the territory of modern-day Saudi Arabia might have been seen to be less valuable than a relatively small portion of the English countryside. Now we might think rather differently given what we know about the natural resources beneath the Saudi Arabian desert. Similarly, large areas of territory do not seem to be of much value either in terms of agriculture or natural resources. How much of the territory of modern-day Niger is equal to a portion of modern-day Massachusetts? So the egalitarian interpretation involves an indeterminacy which makes it implausible as a way of salvaging Locke's claim. Yet there is a further potentially fatal indeterminacy that renders this egalitarian interpretation and the sufficiency account of the constraint inadequate. We have only considered the problem of acquisition in circumstances of a small number of co-existing individuals. Yet the claim of right must apply to all individuals at whatever time they exist. Suppose the initial individuals succeeded in distributing equal shares of the world, that would still deny all subsequent generations access to '. . . enough and as good . . .' of the world's territory of resources. But as we have seen, into which generation one is born should not affect one's rights. Thus Locke's argument seems to be incoherent. The implication some commentators have wished to draw from this is that we can revert to a conventional account of property rights which can be varied according to social need, or more radically that we should instead accept that we have a joint common right to the world which can only be enjoyed with the consent of all others. This latter claim is made by G. A. Cohen. Yet we might actually save Locke from these criticisms. Firstly we should note that Locke does not actually claim that we have a Natural Right to an amount of private property. Throughout the *Second Treatise* his argument is clearly for a right to acquire property through labour, as an extension of the Natural Right to liberty. In addition we can see that when the '. . . enough and as good . . .' condition is mentioned in § 27, Locke's concern is primarily to claim that acquisition should not harm the interests of others. Thus initial acquisition is permissible and legitimate when others are not prevented from also acquiring the means of their own subsistence and preservation. Now as long as we remember that this argument is supposed to apply in the primitive condition of the State of Nature, which is effectively a world of plenty, and that the acquisition is limited by the genuine Natural Law requirement against spoilage, it does not appear quite such a restriction of initial acquisition.

One might argue that this reading still leaves open the challenge of a literal reading of the '. . . enough and as good . . .' constraint. But while we cannot just pick and choose which bits of Locke's argument to accept, we should not read this clause against the grain of the rest of Locke's argument. If the sufficiency claim would restrict the possibility of acquisition short of leaving as much and as good for all mankind, then Locke's argument would entail that we cannot take anything from the common stock to secure our preservation and subsistence. This would effectively entail that we had a duty to starve and that is clearly contrary to all that Locke claims about the most fundamental obligation of the Law of Nature. So either Locke was hopelessly confused and contradicted himself or we need a more charitable interpretation of the '. . . enough and as good . . .' condition. This more charitable interpretation can be found if we do not interpret the claim in the stringent form of the sufficiency claim. Instead we should see Locke's account of the right to private property as a special implication of the more general right to subsistence that follows from the Natural Law. In the primitive state the right to subsistence is perfectly compatible with acquiring exclusive use of land and the produce of labour (subject to its non-spoilage) as there is plenty left for others to secure their own subsistence. It is also clear that Locke thought that even in his own day there was sufficient unused land in the recently discovered North American colonies to support a population greater than that which currently existed. In this way we can see that the point is to show that the prospects of securing individual subsistence are not harmed by the taking of un-owned land; consequently his claim is that no one has a claim of right to prevent another doing so. So just as the taking of what someone else has produced by their labour would be unjust when the expropriator could also have secured his subsistence by labouring, so Locke is arguing that it would be unjust to deprive another of the land they have taken when that does not limit the ability of others to secure their own subsistence. Individual takings might well prevent everyone enjoying the same level of well-being, but that is not part of Locke's argument and there is no Natural Law basis for claiming that everyone has a right to equal well-being. One implication of this argument is that in circumstances where the subsistence of others is prevented by the existing system of property and that there is no other way of securing subsistence, the primary obligation to pre-serve ourselves and others will trump the claims of private property. Yet before this is seen to open the door to socialist redistribution, we should note that Locke's argument refers to the gravest moral cata-strophes that would result in the death of the propertyless. He is cer-tainly not claiming that the poor as such have a claim on the property of others – other than as a matter of charity. We should also note that while Locke is a staunch defender of the claims of private property, in all those places where he describes the threat to property he sees it coming from unconstrained Executive power and not the claims of the helpless and starving.

The invention of money

The claims for non-harmful acquisition are made primarily in a primitive situation and do not continue into the development of civil and political society, so Locke does not really have to deal with the problem of what happens when all the land in England is acquired and there are future generations. The reason he is able to avoid this problem is the invention of money.

The invention of money and the convention to accept metal or pre-cious stones as things of persisting value which can be hoarded or exchanged for goods, marks one of the stages of the emergence of society prior to the creation of political society. The convention that underpins the exchange of precious metal is the most important aspect of Locke's argument as it reintroduces the idea of agreement and consent into the account of property. The reason that money is a convention is that the practice of accepting precious tokens precedes the idea of a general agreement. In other words it is a practice that grows up among people but without any conscious agreement to begin it. Once the practice is in place then consent to the use of money provides its justification, but it is important to note that the form of consent we find here is tacit (§ 50). No one can be compelled to accept tokens in exchange for produce, but once people recognize the value of the convention of money they have good reason to consent to it.

The chief value of money in the first instance is that it enables accumulation that would otherwise fall foul of the non-spoilage constraint. Once accumulation is possible then so is the social surplus that is necessary for the development of society, industry, culture and the arts. Money liberates the power of labour from the satisfaction of immediate need, by allowing labourers to produce objects for sale in return for the conditions of subsistence. Locke alludes to the enormous potential liberated from labour by the invention of money when he contrasts the level of economic development of North America with Europe in § 48.

Alongside the liberation of labour from the mere production of necessaries for subsistence, the invention of money has two important implications for the rest of Locke's argument. In the first instance, money solves the problem of acquisition for subsequent generations, for even if the whole cultivable world were appropriated each person would still have one source of property that could secure subsistence, namely their labour power. Because individuals can still sell their labour in return for wages they effectively have an equal access to the acquisition of property. This does not of course mean that they have a right to the same amount of property, but it does mean that no person can be without property as they can always labour for another in return for wages. Marxist scholars have tended to see Locke's argument as one step on the slippery slope to the alienation and exploitation of the wage-labour system in advanced capitalist societies and therefore see Locke's argument as complicit in the coercion of the liberal state. Yet other scholars have taken a more sympathetic view of Locke's argument on the grounds that his emphasis on labour and the cash economy is part of an assault on aristocracy and landed power. Locke's emphasis on wage labour and movable property following the invention of money is contrasted with the lesser importance he attaches to real property in land after the creation of civil society, and this is perhaps a sign of a move to a more democratic and less aristocratic conception of politics.

The other important implication of the invention of money is that it introduces the legitimacy of material inequality. In tacitly consenting to the acceptance of imperishable tokens in return for goods we are effectively liberating the motive to accumulate more than we need, which is restricted in the primitive condition by the difficulty of labour and the non-spoilage condition. By making possible legitimate accumulation over and above what is needed for subsistence, money makes significant material inequalities possible. But Locke's point is not merely about the possibility of material inequality; his point is also about the legitimacy of material inequality. Inequalities are justified because we have tacitly consented to them through the system that makes them possible. While we continue to use and accept money we continue to consent to those inequalities. Locke's argument in support of this claim seems to be that we could still reject the use of money if we wished and therefore our not doing so is a sign of consent. But furthermore, his claim that accumulation and the liberation of labour power have created so many of the good things of society suggests that there is a utilitarian dimension to his argument. We consent, albeit tacitly, because the monetary system brings with it considerable benefits for all of us, even the worst off, as it allows for the accumulation of a surplus that makes charity possible.

What Locke does not consider is whether this tacit consent is free or coerced and this is because he does not consider the extent to which the wage labour and the monetary system entrenches unequal distributions of power and advantage that are just as arbitrary as the arbitrary power he saw in political absolutism. It is precisely this concern that inspires both Jean-Jacques Rousseau's and Karl Marx's critiques of the system of private property that is made possible by the wage labour system. Locke has no theoretical understanding of economic power and its coercive potential. Many subsequent commentators have used this apparent failure as a general criticism of liberal political theories. Whether Locke was indifferent to the arbitrariness of economic power can only remain a matter of speculation. It is not however obvious that all liberal theories must be tainted by this apparent weakness and that they must regard economic inequality and all its consequences as either legitimate or else an indifferent matter.

Property and colonial acquisition

There is one final dimension of Locke's argument that is worth commenting on because of his involvement in North American colonization and because of some recent arguments raised by defenders of aboriginal land claims in Canada and Australia about the liberal and Western notion of property that we find in Locke and other seventeenth-century thinkers who provided the justification for that colonial expansion and exploitation.

Locke defended the rights of colonists to take from the unused stock of the North American wilderness and to subdue it through labour. As the colonists were exercising their rights to acquire from the common stock they were acting within the Law of Nature. Consequently, if Native Americans attempt to throw the settlers off the land and destroy their smallholdings, then Locke would argue they are engaged in unlawful aggression and the settlers are therefore within their rights to go to war against the Native Americans. Locke provided Just War arguments to defend the extension of colonial administration into North America on the grounds that the Native Americans forfeited their rights through interfering with the just acquisition of un-owned land. How far these were Locke's arguments and not merely arguments he developed for others need not concern us here. The real issue arises with subsequent generations of Native Americans who claim that the land that was settled was actually expropriated. They might argue for instance that the land may have looked un-used or un-owned but was actually traditional hunting grounds that supplied a whole people. Locke's argument not only has no place for such group claims but it also seems to provide arguments against recognizing them.

As we have seen, Locke's basic account of initial acquisition includes the enclosure and cultivation of land. To argue that a forest is a collective resource enjoyed by a whole people has no power to preclude individual ownership. At best the collective claim is to the products of the forest – the deer and other game caught there. Locke would have to deny that the group claim could extend to exclusive use of a forest or territory for a particular type of activity. Indeed he was not particularly impressed by claims to enclose parks in England for the exclusive use of hunting by the aristocracy. Locke clearly has a particular conception of property-conferring use in mind in his theory, and this precludes the kinds of cultural use claimed by first nations or tribal bands. It has been claimed by some recent commentators that the prevalence of this 'Lockean' or liberal conception of property has done much to hinder the claims of aboriginal peoples in the quest for just recognition of their land claims.

iv PATRIARCHAL POWER AND THE FAMILY

Since the opening section of the *Second Treatise*, Locke has been keen to reject patriarchal theories of political power and authority. His strongest argument against patriarchalists such as Filmer is that their theories are incoherent for either there are as many kings as fathers if kingly power is a species of patriarchal power or else we do not owe obedience to our real fathers, in which case the patriachalist theory clearly flies in the face of scriptural commandments. Although Locke rejected the patriachalist theory of political power he did not deny that there was such a thing as paternal power and thus he needed to explain how it fitted into his account of Natural Law and Natural Right. §§ 52–86 provide an extended discussion of the family, children and the 'natural' subordination of women. The material covered in these sections is important to Locke as it further supports his distinction between political and other forms of power, but it is also important because it raises a number of apparent problems with his account of law and rights which he wanted to address directly. Finally from our modern perspective, Locke's argument has been seen to reinforce the subjection of women and even the denial of their fundamental equality with men. He has also been seen as a defender of a strict liberal separation between the public and the private sphere, which places the family and conjugal relations beyond public and political scrutiny. This feminist critique has been addressed at Locke directly, but also at social contract arguments of the kind that Locke popularized. As we shall see, Locke's argument is more subtle than it is often given credit for; he was certainly radical by the standards of his own day. That said, he is not an early twenty-first-century feminist. However, before we dismiss this concern with the status of women as an alien concern to a seventeenth-century philosopher, we should note that Locke opened the discussion of paternal power (§ 52) by acknowledging that it should more properly be called parental power. Paternal power '. . . seems to place the Power of Parents over their Children wholly in the *Father*, as if the *Mother* had no share in it, whereas if we consult Reason or Revelation, we shall find she hath an equal Title'. Locke also refers to the biblical commandment to honour one's father and mother to show that the natural authority of parents acknowledged in scripture is jointly shared and not conferred on men alone. We have here an indication that Locke acknowledged some claim to gender equality within the family, even if he seems to retract that later on. Yet his point is not to defend gender equality – which he does not do. Instead he is concerned to show how an imprecise use of language has supported the patriarchalist's conflation of paternal and political authority. If paternal authority is properly understood to include the authority of mothers and fathers, then the supposed analogy with kingly authority quickly evaporates, not least because the idea of unitary sovereignty in the hands of the king is clearly divided and shared by parents within the family. Divided and shared sovereignty is the last thing that the patriarchalists claimed to be defending.

But if paternal power is not like political power we still need some account of it which explains its origins and its relationship to political power. This explanatory account needs to take account of the natural and pre-political dimensions of the family and paternal power, but it must also reconcile the claims of natural authority and institutions with his account of the legitimacy of dominion or power in terms of Natural Law and Natural Rights. Locke is careful to separate the issues of explanation and legitimation in addressing the issue of authority within the family as he knew that if he conceded too much to natural authority he would re-open the door to those theories, such as Filmer's, that claimed that political subjection was natural. Yet if Locke asserted that even in the family the only legitimate source of authority was consent and agreement he faced a challenge posed by children to his account of freedom and equality.

The status of children
The first premise of Locke's theory of Natural Rights is that '. . . all Men by Nature are equal' and it is in virtue of this equality that they can only be subjected to the dominion of another by consent or agreement. This claim to fundamental equality is a normative or ethical claim. As Locke goes on to acknowledge in § 54, this equality of right is perfectly consistent with some being natural unequals, or what he calls people varying in terms of 'excellence of parts' or merit. By this he means that some people are stronger or brighter than others. The realism of the claim for normative equality is precisely what is asserted by patriarchalists who remind us that we are born weak and subject to our parents and not as some kind of fully grown natural equals. The rejection of the realism of the premise of fundamental equality is used as a basis for challenging its normative

force. If one can make the claim of natural equality seem descriptively naive, it seems less persuasive as a moral claim. This is a standard challenge to egalitarian theories throughout the history of political thought and to State of Nature arguments.

Locke might well have responded to the sceptics by arguing that children are not natural equals but are nevertheless moral equals as rights bearers, yet in § 55 this is precisely what he denies. He says 'Children, I confess are not born in this full state of Equality, though they are born to it'. The reason for this concession is to be found in the account of fundamental equality that we considered in the discussion of the State of Nature. Persons are equals in the relevant sense when they share the 'range-property' of rationality and agency. Infant children do not share this 'range-property' at all when they are born, as they cannot speak or reason; consequently they cannot be our moral equals. Locke suggests that only the biblical character of Adam came into the world fully formed and therefore fully under the Law of Nature. All other men will have been born into subjection until the natural capacity to reason has developed. Locke likens the natural dominion of parents over children to the subjection of 'Swadling Cloths' in which infants were traditionally wrapped. As the child grows the bonds are loosened so in the case of the cultivation of reason and the move to full maturity. Once a child's capacity to reason is fully developed and he or she is able to understand the natural Law of Reason then the authority of parents over children disappears. Most societies have conventions concerning when majority is reached and when children can be held responsible for their actions as agents. Yet Locke's point is more fundamental as it assumes that once the individual capacity to reason is developed an individual ceases to be under the legitimate rule of a parent, whatever the convention of a society happens to be. In the case of some human individuals such as 'Lunaticks and Ideots', this minimal capacity to reason is never achieved and they must remain under the rule of their parents throughout their life. Those who are permanently mentally incapacitated are not strictly full human persons, nor are they potential persons as they may never be able to exhibit the 'range-property' of reason and agency.

In order to be a moral agent individuals need to achieve a level of rational comprehension of the world and their place in it. It is for this reason that Locke does not just assume that human beings are moral equals as a matter of natural fact: he does argue that individuals are born with the capacity to be free rational agents, but he distinguishes between this capacity and the exercise of the capacity. It is the exercise of the capacity that matters; indeed without that evidence we would never know whether someone had the capacity. Normative or ethical status is an achievement that can admit of degrees, but it does mean that some apparent humans who never demonstrate the ability to exercise the capacity are never fully human in the ethical sense. This class of human fits more properly into the same class as animals or other aspects of non-human nature. This might seem a troubling account of our moral relations to the mentally incapacitated by our modern standards – although Locke's claim that such 'people' should be subjected to the authority of their family might well have been more humane than many seventeenth-century practices for dealing with the mentally ill or incapacitated – yet it is more pressing for the role and status of all human infants, all of whom would fall outside the realm of moral concern at the most vulnerable period of their lives.

We will see how Locke tries to address this problem in just a moment, but before turning to the basis of parents' duties towards their children, it is important to note two things. Firstly, the idea that the capacity for reason is something that develops and can be nurtured explains the importance of education in Locke's broader philosophical system where questions of learning, education and the nature and conditions of knowledge play such an important role. It also explains the importance of education and the cultivation of the intellect in the subsequent liberal tradition. Secondly, we should note one important implication of Locke's claim that nobody can be under a law or obligation that they cannot understand (§ 57) for his account of the Law of Nature. Although Locke does not draw out the implication of this claim at this point, it has an important role in terms of qualifying the theological dimensions of his Law of Nature and in illustrating that the Law of Nature must be distinguished from Divine Law based on special revelation. In Locke's later work he goes to considerable lengths to show how his account of the Law of Nature is consistent with Christian Divine Law, but he is also clear that we should not reduce one to the other. For most of human existence and in most of the world during Locke's time, people would have been ignorant of Christian revelation of the Bible. Locke was indeed concerned about this matter and endeavoured to show that reason on its own could provide us with some understanding of the basis of morality and our obligations to and rights against others. This is why he identifies the capacity of reason as the 'range-property' that distinguishes our membership of the moral community. Consequently, we should not read too much of Locke's own Christian moral commitments into his political and ethical theory, as he clearly did not want to claim that our obligations depend upon each individual knowing the Bible. Whatever God intended us to do as a matter of strict obligation must therefore be available to each person's knowledge and intellect.

The duty of parents and the role of the family

We have just seen that Locke argues that children are not moral equals and therefore are outside of the Law of Nature and not the bearers of Natural Rights against all other men. If this is so we might wonder why parents should not simply be free to kill their children or treat them as mere objects of nature beyond the law, such as rocks, plants or animals. Parents cannot therefore be under a duty not to kill their children, at least not one that is based on the rights of the children. Yet Locke also claims that parents have a duty of care towards their children and it is on the basis of this duty that they claim power over their children. So where does this duty come from? The simple answer is that parents have an obligation to nurture and protect their children as a result of the basic Natural Law to preserve others as much as possible. So the needless destruction of infants is ruled out by the duty to preserve. But there are two points we should note here: firstly, the duty is a general duty and not based on any special moral claim that children can make; secondly, the duty falls on everyone and not solely upon parents. Parents have a special responsibility on the basis of proximity, but nothing more. Indeed Locke acknowledges this when he argues that the obligation extended equally to foster parents and other remote relatives, and more importantly when he recognizes that the responsibility of care for children falls on both parents and not just mothers. It is interesting to note also that Locke explicitly denies the idea that parents have an ownership right in children because they expend labour and effort in their creation. Children are not the 'workmanship' of their parents – only God can claim a right to ownership of human beings on the basis of their being his workmanship. As we saw in the discussion of property, Locke rejects the idea that individuals are full self-owners and therefore they cannot claim full ownership of their offspring.

The question at issue is not one of special rights and duties. Children do not have a right to care from their parents, as they have no rights to anything until they reach the age of majority, at which point parental authority evaporates and becomes illegitimate. Similarly parents do not have a special duty to their children other than a duty to preserve what has been created. As we have seen this could in principle fall on anyone, and does fall on non-biological parents in the event of the death of a father or mother. It therefore seems that in principle we could establish collective or social child-rearing as the best way to nurture and preserve children, yet Locke rejects this in favour of attaching special significance to the family. The family is important in Locke's theory, both as an institution through which child care and nurture is provided, and as an institution that is prior to the introduction of political society and authority. This still leaves the question of why the family is special and why parents have special duties and primary responsibility for children.

Locke's answer to this question is interesting as he turns away from the language of rights and duties and towards the language of sentiment that was to play such an important role in eighteenth-century philosophy and the move towards utilitarianism. He wrote

> God hath made it their business to imploy this Care on their Off-spring, and hath placed in them suitable Inclinations of Tenderness and Concern to temper this power, to apply it as his Wisdom designed it, to the Childrens good, as long as they should need be under it. (§ 63)

Locke explained the source of this motivation in God's design of our nature, but the more important point of the argument is that the obligation and duty of special concern for offspring are found in our natural inclinations. This argument prefigures the turn towards sentiment as an explanation of morality in later thinkers of the eighteenth century, and in some way it prefigures the naturalistic psychology that underpins utilitarianism. What he does as well, however, is open up the possibility of an account of moral obligations that extends beyond the boundaries of traditional Natural Law. For if some of our responsibilities are based on natural sentiments then the ability to exercise reason is not the sole criterion for moral relevance. Locke does not develop this argument and he certainly does not wish to replace the rationalist account of Natural Rights with a naturalistic ethic of sentiment. But it is interesting to note here, and as we shall see with his account of tacit consent, that he is opening up avenues of enquiry that many of his later critics were to exploit in the move from Natural Law to utilitarianism.

The crucial point to remember here is that Locke is not deriving duties from this natural inclination; instead he is appealing to it to explain why parents feel a responsibility for their own children and, more importantly, why the family is an important social institution. Again he is separating the causal motives to act in a certain way from the account of our obligations. Parents have a natural claim of first responsibility because they feel this responsibility more strongly than others and it is a good thing that they do. Consequently we have a kind of utilitarian justification for the primary claim of the family in child-rearing on the grounds that the benefits that it brings establishes its claim to respect. The family is definitely a good thing for Locke and it is also a primitive natural society that can be found in earliest times. However, Locke's naturalistic defence of the value of the family and the primacy of parents in caring for and nurturing children remains qualified by his commitment to Natural Law. Although parents have a natural (God-given) sentiment of concern for their children, it can only provide a temporary justification of the subjection of children. Once children achieve the age of majority, whatever that happens to be, they acquire the full enjoyment of the Natural Rights and this exempts them from subjection to the authority of their parents. This is another way in which Locke thinks the patriarchalist confusion of paternal and political power fails. If children were not free from paternal power on the age of majority they could never exercise political power as this would always revert to their parents. And as Locke has shown that paternal power is exercised as much by mothers (indeed more so) as by fathers: all kings would have to defer to their mothers. Once again this is not a particularly attractive conclusion for the patriarchal absolutist such as Filmer.

The obligations of children and parents

Parents do not have strict obligations towards their children, but Locke does claim that they have a natural primary inclination to care for and nurture their offspring. Most of the discussion of this inclination concerns the provision of sustenance to infants, but

Locke does not confine parental concern to basic animal sustenance. He also refers to the parent's duty to discipline and educate his offspring – what he sometimes refers to as a right of tuition (§ 67). Education as we have seen matters because it is important in cultivating the ability to exercise the power of reason and free agency. This duty to educate is an alienable right and one that terminates once the child is educated. Locke does not set a clear limit to what counts as being educated but one can readily assume that he has a sufficiency criterion which is fulfilled by the minimal competency to exercise rational agency. The responsibility to educate can also be alienated to another person as illustrated by the example of apprenticeship (§ 69) or presumably schooling. During the period of the apprenticeship the parental right to rule a child passes to the apprentice master or school master and it is only in such cases that the right to discipline can be distinguished from arbitrary third-party violence. The parent has the first responsibility of care for his children, whereas the second responsibility of the apprentice master or teacher will be derived from an agreement between the adults concerned and not based on natural inclination or sentiment. Although the natural motive of parents cannot be alienated, the substantive duty can. In the case of education there is no special role for biological connections between the teacher and pupil. The parent fulfils his role by providing education, whether this is exercised by him or on his behalf by someone more qualified.

Finally, although the parent does have some obligation towards his children, he is not under an obligation to leave his property to his children. There is a widespread convention that grounds the expectation of children to inherit the property of their fathers. Locke does appear to endorse this convention and the weight of expectation, but he is clear that the right to inherit is merely a liberty right (he has no duty NOT to receive an inheritance) and not a claim. A parent is perfectly permitted to determine how his property should be divided among his children and he is perfectly within his discretion to reward children as he sees fit and in accordance with their obedience and assistance.

While the responsibilities of parents to children are time-limited and alienable, the responsibilities of children to parents are not. One might wonder why Locke even thinks that there are such responsibilities to parents, as once a child has reached the age of majority he can only be subject to parental authority by his own consent. The simple answer is to be found in the biblical injunction to honour one's father and mother. This is a clear injunction in the Bible and it seems to be supported by natural and conventional sentiments in many societies and cultures.

Much of Locke's discussion of the duty of honour to parents (§§ 66–76) is concerned with qualifying its claims so that it cannot be used as a basis for a patriarchal right to rule children or a ground for a substantial filial duty from children to their parents. As we have seen there are no real filial rights because, prior to majority, a parent's right to rule is not based on any duty to children as they are not rights bearers; once they become rights bearers the only duties they have to parents are based on consent. Locke re-emphasizes this point within his discussion of the duty to honour by arguing that this duty to parents does not establish a right to command children and most importantly it does not entitle parents to any portion of a child's property or wealth. Children have a duty to honour their parents and support them on the grounds that they have supported and nurtured them while young. The obligation appears to be one of reciprocity on the grounds that parents have brought children into the world and enabled them to become free agents. The honour of parents involves some fairly straightforward restraints from actions that would harm or injure their life or happiness. Locke also speaks of '. . . relief, assistance and comfort . . .' (§ 66) but this is far from a justification for submitting children to the rule of parents or giving parents a right to the life, liberty and property of their children. The duty to honour parents does not give parents a power to alter the rights of a child who has attained maturity, nor does it restrict the liberty or discretion of the child to decide how they should honour their parents. Finally, the degree of honour due is variable in proportion to the level of concern and support a parent has shown to a child in exercising the parents' duty of care and tuition. Locke does not go so far as absolving a child of honour towards abusive parents but he does allow for the possibility of very minimal obligations of honour when he writes '. . . the degrees of what is required of Children, may be varied, by the different care and kindness, trouble and expence, which is often imployed upon one Child . . .' (§ 70). All of these qualifications are important because they further undermine the derivation of political power from paternal power. If we were to deduce one from another, then according to Locke we might end up with variable political obligations between subjects depending upon how well they had been treated by the king, but more importantly we would have a minimal duty not to harm or injure the king and no obligation to subject our person, liberty or property to his rule. We do not accept these rights towards parents so why would we accept them with respect to kings? The answer would have to be different to that derived from a duty of honour to parents.

Locke concludes his discussion of the confusion of paternal and political power with an interesting historical or anthropological speculation about how the confusion of ideas arose (§§ 74–6). He argues that in more primitive societies the role of parents, and particularly fathers, was closely identified with that of rulers. Fathers would have tended to exercise the Executive power of the Law of Nature on behalf of children and families, thus giving the appearance of exercising a right to punish up to the infliction of death. However, Locke is clear that this confusion of paternal and political power is in appearance only; after all, the Executive power of the Law of Nature and the duty to punish can be exercised by any mature adult, so even here the conflation of paternal and political rule is a matter of functional convenience and not one of legitimacy. Fathers have no more rights in this respect than anyone else. Mischievously, Locke reinforces the point about the limits of deducing any normative claims from the practice of primitive societies, by arguing that fathers can also be seen to exercise the function of priests. Patriachalist theorists, such as Filmer, would certainly not have wanted to conflate the power of fathers, kings and priests, as most of the conservative supporters of patriarchal absolutism would also have been strong supporters of episcopal governance of churches and as such strong defenders of the rights of bishops as distinct from those of princes.

The conjugal or sexual contract

Locke's discussion of the family continues into the next chapter on the origins Of Political or Civil Society (Chapter VII). The discussion begins with a familiar argument from the history of political thought about the origins of the most simple forms of human society; we can find this in Aristotle and most political philosophers since his time. On this view the first society is found between a man and wife and concerns the propagation of the species and their care. In the few short sections from §§ 77–84, Locke extends the discussion of the family from that of parents' responsibility to children to the internal governance of the family. In these sections Locke explains the basis for the widespread gendered division of labour in the family that existed during his lifetime and which still characterizes the relations between men and women today. For many subsequent feminist readers and critics of Locke, his refutation of patriarchal accounts of political power reinforces a more pervasive form of patriarchy in wider social relations. These critics, such as Carole Pateman in her influential book *The Sexual Contract*,[20] have gone on to argue that the whole tradition of social contract thinking that has its roots in Locke's *Second Treatise* masks the persistent oppression and domination of women. The sexual contract that Pateman refers to is the conjugal contract found in § 78 of Locke's argument, which explains the nature of, and authority within, the family. The point of Locke's argument is that conjugal society is based on contract or agreement and therefore any inequality of power, authority or right is based on the agreement of both parties. The point of the feminist critique is to show that the conjugal contract reflects a pre-contractual natural subordination of women to men. To examine this charge let us begin with Locke's account of conjugal society.

In the previous section on paternal power Locke explained how the obligation of parents to children was based on a natural inclination to care for and nurture offspring. That explanation accounts for why individual parents care for their offspring, but it does not explain why this should give rise to a certain kind of society, namely the family. Locke turns to this issue in § 78 where he argues that conjugal society between male and female parents is based on a voluntary agreement between both parties. Initially this gives rise to access to the body of another, so Locke is clear that sexual relations must be consensual. This condition clearly indicates that rape is a serious violation of rights, but it also suggests an individualistic and liberal conception of marriage or conjugal society. Locke goes on to argue that what began as an issue of what gives one a right to another's body soon becomes a basis for a long-term relationship of mutual assistance. Marriage begins with the demands of sex and procreation, but develops into a complex social relationship of mutual support. As the former dimension cannot be coerced, so by implication the latter cannot be coerced either. Marriage and long-term conjugal society must be based on consent and agreement. For this reason we speak of a marriage and conjugal society as a contract. The length of this relationship should also be governed by the needs of the parties during the birth and nurture of young children. Locke suggests that in some cases nature allows other animals to fulfil the demands of conjugal society merely in the act of procreation. He has in mind grazing animals who once born are almost wholly independent from their fathers. Other 'beasts of prey' depend upon support and protection for much longer. The suggestion seems to be that human animals are much more like the beasts of prey than the 'viviparous Animals which feed on Grass . . .' (§ 79). The reason that the human conjugal society tends to last much longer than that of any other animal is explained by the nature of successive pregnancies leading to large families. It is simply because the needs of the human conjugal society are more complex that they have a much longer duration than any other such society observed in animals. Furthermore, the satisfaction of those needs would be continually disrupted if conjugal society was not kept with the same partner. Nature provides part of the explanation for the emergence and persistence of conjugal society. Locke goes on to acknowledge that once the tasks of procreation and education are complete there is no reason why natural conjugal society should continue. There is in effect no reason other than the existence of positive law which requires that conjugal society continues for life. By implication Locke is acknowledging that there is no reason why the positive law of a political society should not countenance divorce on appropriate terms and more importantly that where conjugal society does persist to the end of life this is because the parties concerned choose that it should. Once again we have a clear understanding of marriage and the family as being based on agreement and consent. The situation becomes more complex in § 82, where Locke discusses governance within the family or conjugal society. The problem arises because of the existence of two distinct wills which can come into conflict in deciding how best to achieve the ends of such society. In a situation of conflict there must be some authority to rule, but Locke goes on to claim '. . . it naturally falls to the Man's share, as the abler and the stronger'. It is this latter claim that has attracted much comment as Locke seems to just accept a convention as the norm for governance within the family, on the basis of inequalities of natural strength. There are a number of issues that we should note here.

1. Locke is not merely following conventional practice of his day as he goes on to explain that convention in terms of natural power.

2. He appears to suggest that the difference of nature is not simply strength but also ability, and this has led some to argue that Locke thinks women are not fully rational, or at least not the rational equals of men.

3. He seems to undercut his own argument by allowing unequal natural power to justify subjection, whereas throughout his argument thus far he has distinguished between our physical natures and our moral natures under the Law of Nature. He has distinguished between explanation and legitimation. In this case he seems to confuse the two.

On the issue of convention, it is clear that Locke is not simply following the conventions of his day, as his account of the family as based on that mutual advantage to both parties is an important departure from seventeenth-century conventions about the natural-ness of women's subordination to men. This is reinforced by Locke's claim following the passage just quoted, that it does not give any right to the property or estate of the women. To this extent Locke's argument poses a significant challenge to many of the prejudices of his own day, including legal restrictions on wives holding property independently of their husbands' control. Locke is no twenty-first-century feminist, but we should be careful in judging him too harshly by such standards.

On the charge that Locke suggests that women are less rational than men it is clear that this is an unnaturally forced reading of his argument. As we have just seen, Locke does maintain that women can be property holders and therefore are rights bearers, unlike children. Even if Locke thought that women were less rational than men, and he might well have thought this about some women, this would still not deny them equality of rights according to his account of rationality as a 'range-property'. For Locke, some women, such as Damaris Masham, may well have been the intellectual superiors of many men, whereas other women were clearly the inferiors. That said, there is a threshold beneath which persons need to drop before they cease to be the minimal moral equals that fall within the Law of Nature. There is nothing to suggest that Locke held all women as a class to fall below that threshold.

All of that being said, there is still one ground on which Locke's acceptance of patriarchal conjugal relations is definitely subject to the feminist challenge. This is the ideal that a convention based on natural inequality provides a legitimate basis for subjection of women to men. One may challenge the empirical claim that women are naturally weaker than men, or at least all men. Some women will undoubtedly be stronger than some men, but that is not really the point. The central issue is whether the fact of natural inequality can create legitimate subjection. All of the arguments so far in the *Second Treatise* reject the idea of natural power as a basis for subjection. If Locke does not hold to this premise then he would be conceding that anyone with the power could impose their will and become legitimate, and this would allow a Catholic monarch such as James II to rule legitimately as long as he had enough French troops to impose his will. The feminist critics' argument is therefore a very good one, for if Locke allows natural inequality as grounds for subjection anywhere, then he must allow it everywhere, or else provide a convincing argument about why women are a special case. As we have just seen he does not provide a clear-cut argument that women are a special case.

In defence of Locke, one might argue that he is basing the subjection of women within the family on consent, so there is no problem. But this is precisely where the problem does arise according to the feminist, for one can consent at the point of a sword (to paraphrase Thomas Hobbes) and one can submit oneself to another because one has no realistic choice or option, or because the threat of coercion makes one self-censor and not express one's disagreement with the terms of the contract. This is the fundamental claim of the feminists. If power is already disproportionately with men because they control access to opportunities and resources, then any agreement will merely reflect the unequal bargaining position of the parties concerned. Just as we should not accept that a person handing their wallet to a highwayman is consenting to the property transfer, because of the coercive imposition of his pistol, so we should not accept any agreement that takes place against an unfair base-line or natural inequality or political coercion. Given that many women will actually be physically stronger than many men, we should be suspicious of claims that the near universal gendered distribution of domestic labour and responsibility as well as the subordination of women to the governance of their husbands, follows a natural tendency amongst rational women to seek their protection and advantage at the hands of men. Instead it might simply reflect the pervasive influence of patriarchal domination of women by men.

Before one dismisses these criticisms of Locke as the imposition of contemporary political values on the seventeenth century, we should note that in Locke's own day writers such as Mary Astell were already beginning to draw attention to the plight of women and that by the later part of the eighteenth century Mary Wollstonecraft was developing a rights-based argument for women's social and political equality.

The feminist challenge raises a more fundamental point about the nature of Locke's conception of equality and rights, that has troubled subsequent thinkers of a liberal and radical persuasion. This is the argument that unless basic rights are enjoyed above a threshold of social and material equality (liberals and radicals argue about how great that equality must be), then they are equals in name only, and their rights provide no protection against domination and exploitation. Among contemporary liberals this problem has given rise to the primacy of social justice or some conception of a fair basic structure which would guarantee that any exercise of individual rights, such as the right to enter into conjugal society, is never coerced by individual actions of economic necessity. How far Locke's argument can go in addressing or challenging claims about social justice or structural inequalities would take us beyond the remit of a book like this, but it is worth noting on this issue, as on so many others, how Locke addresses or exposes problems that are still current in our own politics.

v THE ORIGINS OF POLITICAL SOCIETY

Locke's argument thus far has been to distinguish the idea of political rule and authority from paternal rule and the despotical rule of slave-holders. In each case the contrast is to show how the patriarchalist defence of absolutist political rule involves a category mistake by confusing one kind of authority for another. Yet this emphasis on the distinction of legitimate rule from other kinds of authority and illegitimate forms of political rule leaves open the question of whether Locke's account of legitimate political rule could actually arise in the real world. To this end, Locke sets out to show how his idea of a constitutionally limited state could arise and then to show how this account can be seen to operate in history. Locke's argument in this section is a hypothetical contract argument, but it is not just that, as we shall see.

The original contract

The first question that Locke's account of the origin of the state is supposed to answer is the anarchist's question – why do we need a state at all? The anarchist's challenge is particularly important in Locke's case as, unlike Hobbes or other pessimistic contractarians, he does concede the idea of society prior to the artificial creation of civil or political society. We have already seen that Locke acknowledges the pre-political nature of the family and by implication the idea of clan or tribal societies prior to the creation of the modern state. Similarly we have seen that the State of Nature includes complex social practices that evolve around the idea of private property such as money and exchange. All of these social practices entail conventions and rules which are independent of the idea of a single sovereign power. But most importantly, Locke's State of Nature is not a war of all against all, but is rather a law-governed order where people already have rights, duties and obligations and the executive power to punish their violation. For the anarchist all of this might well seem sufficient. What more is added by the creation of sovereign political power?

To answer this we need to go back to the idea of the Executive power of the Law of Nature that is central to Locke's account of the State of Nature. In the State of Nature each person has the Executive power to enforce and punish breaches of the Law of Nature. But as we saw earlier in § 13 the equal right to exercise this Executive power entails a number of inconveniences that are the result of human partiality and passion. The problem is that if everyone is effectively judge, jury and executioner of the Law of Nature there is no impartial judge who can arbitrate between disputes about the application of the law and the appropriate level of just punishment, when it is breached. The origin of political or civil society – which in Locke's case and contrary to contemporary usage mean the same thing – is the rational desire to impose a single impartial judge between men in disputes about their rights. The task of the state is to legislate so that individual rights might be given a clear and determinate application through settled laws that apply to all, and to execute the application of those laws when there is a dispute between persons. The point of Locke's original contract then is to establish government to overcome the inconveniences of the State of Nature. Yet Locke's account of the origin of civil and political society has two stages. The first stage is the establishment of a political community. The second stage concerns the establishment of government and we will return to that in the next section.

Let us begin by exploring Locke's account of the origin of political society. In § 95 Locke claims that a political community originates when a group of men agree '. . . with other Men to joyn and unite into a Community, for their comfortable, safe, and peaceable living one amongst another, in a secure Enjoyment of their Properties, and a greater Security against any that are not of it.' So the initial stage involves joining into one body politic or a particular community that previously did not exist. The first point to note about this is that Locke claims that political society unlike other forms of society – tribal, clan, family – is a voluntary association. Nobody who does not agree to join the political society can be coerced to fall under its rule. But as we saw in the explanation of Locke's preoccupation with real property in land, the idea of a civil society is not merely an abstract community of people who agree to recognize each other as members. We could for example consider a large number of dispersed individuals to agree and accept an authority, such as that of a church or religion, yet claim that this does not entail territorial concentration or limited jurisdiction. Indeed one of Locke's concerns about Roman Catholicism was not so much its doctrinal content, but its claim to universal jurisdiction.[21] Locke's conception of a political society is a bounded territorial jurisdiction, where the boundaries are set by the limits of the property held by the respective members of that society. So one of the essential features of the origin of a political community is the pooling of property into one territorially constituted political community. This explains why there are particular political communities, for unless people join their property together there can be no political community. As the point of pooling property into a territorially constituted political community is its protection through legislation, the primary need for protection will be from those who are proximate rather than those who are wholly remote. There is no developmental logic in Locke's theory towards a world state as there is no obvious threat that a world state provides unique protection against. It is this emphasis on property and territoriality which further distinguishes Locke's theory of Natural Law from those of his predecessors such as Aquinas. The idea of security of property and the equal protection of the laws can be provided by any state of sufficient size that it is not immediately threatened by an outsider, whether individual or state.

It is important to note, however, that in speaking of pooling property into a single political community or body politic, Locke does not argue that individuals alienate (or give away) their private property to the community, as his contemporary Samuel Pufendorf had argued. Locke's point is that we merely transfer our right to execute the Law of Nature with respect to our property, but retain full original ownership of that property. What Locke does not concede is that the political community acquires a power of eminent domain over everyone's property. We do not merely have individual possession in the State of Nature which is then turned into private property by the creation of a sovereign legislator; we actually have and retain full ownership from the State of Nature into civil society. The point of pooling our property is merely that it marks the boundary of the jurisdiction of the state in enforcing and securing property. The state or political community has no jurisdiction in adjudicating disputes between those within civil society and those without. The political society can protect members against outsiders, but cannot decide upon the legitimacy of property held by outsiders. It is for this reason that Locke argues that a ruler of one state exists in a State of Nature with an individual from another political society (§ 14).

This voluntary association model of political society has continued to prove attractive to subsequent political theorists, but it is not without its difficulties as is acknowledged by one of its foremost contemporary defenders, Robert Nozick.[22] Nozick is particularly exercised by the problem of independents who may find themselves surrounded by the territory of a political society, but who have chosen not to submit to it. Such people can be dealt with easily if they threaten the surrounding members of the political society, but they are a greater problem if they wish to live in peace with the surrounding political community. In effect such independents get the full protection of the new state, but as non-members cannot be required to bear any of the burdens of state membership, such as the cost of administering justice, internal security and defence. Nozick is right to point out that such people would pose a problem for Locke as he is adamant that one can only fall under an obligation to a political society by agreeing to membership in an original contract. As Locke's argument is based on a rational desire to avoid the inconveniences of the State of Nature, he would be bound to accept the legitimacy of free-riding on those who have consented to the burdens of membership of political society.

Nozick's solution to the problem is to draw on ideas of fairness and threat-advantage on the part of the majority of the political community giving a reason to the independents to consent to political rule. These arguments have not persuaded most of Nozick's readers and leave the problem unanswered. As Locke's argument begins from an even more robustly individualist right to private property, he has no argument for compelling the independents to join a particular political society.

That said, although the problem remains in his abstract theory, Locke thought that in reality the problem did not arise because the issue of territorial concentration was largely taken care of in the historical evolution of particular societies. One of the most striking features of the argument in Chapter VIII where he develops his account of the origin of political society is the amount of speculative and biblical history that he draws on to show how political societies develop out of pre-existing clan and tribal societies. He is clear to point out that these historical stories do not establish legitimate political societies, but he is equally clear to show that the point at which the legitimating original contract takes place is a point where territorial concentration has taken place and the problem of independents has disappeared. This does not provide an adequate philosophical response to the problem of conceiving political societies as voluntary associations. Yet Locke is not as vulnerable to the kind of challenge to original contract arguments that one finds in the writings of David Hume, as is commonly suggested. Writing a generation after Locke's death, Hume criticized the idea of an original contractual basis for political society on the grounds of its historical implausibility. There is no historical record of such an original contract and all that we know about the origin of early political communities would tend to contradict Locke's claim. Most societies have their foundation myths, such as the founding of Rome by Romulus and Remus, but no society sees its founding in an original contract.

Yet Locke does not think that the historical record is quite such a problem for his theory. As we have seen, the historical record can provide an alternative account of the concentration of property as we see in scriptural and speculative histories. But remember that Locke's argument is primarily about the legitimacy of political rule, not simply its causal origin. Once property is concentrated in a single political community, and the members of that community acknowledge their governance as a political community, we can see, according to Locke, how political societies can emerge from tribal and clan societies by an act of consent. Although Locke does not use the idea of an unfolding historical process in his account of the origins of political society, we can see how there is an implicit recognition of such a process in explaining the development of society to such a point where it can become a political society. That process must, however, involve the agreement of a property-holder for his property to fall within the jurisdiction of a particular state. As we shall see later, this issue of consent and agreement is not without its difficulties, especially given that Locke argues that it must be free and uncoerced.

However, before moving on to examine the second stage of Locke's account of the origin of political society, we need to consider one further aspect of his account of the territorial jurisdiction of the sovereign state. Although I have noted that in pooling one's property with others to constitute a political community those property rights are not alienated from their original owner to the community, there remains one way in which individual property rights do change. Once property in land has been pooled to form a political community, the members of that community no longer retain a right to secede from that community with their real property in land. If anyone wishes to leave the jurisdiction of a state then they may sell their property and take their movable wealth elsewhere, but they cannot withdraw their land from the territorial jurisdiction of the state.

In the case of subsequent generations, Locke does not think there is much of a problem with the rejection of secession. As we saw in the discussion of parents' rights over their children, Locke does acknowledge one way in which parents may bind their children once they achieve the age of majority and that is through setting the terms of inheritance. Although a child may form a just expectation to inherit his father's property, as that property belongs to his father he can set the terms under which the inheritance is enjoyed. The most obvious condition is that the property is enjoyed as part of the political community in which it is located. Furthermore, as we shall see in the discussion of tacit consent, the acceptance of an inheritance by a child is a sign of an acknowledgement of the legal system in which the property exists; therefore the inheritor consents to being part of a political community. Secession is ruled out for subsequent generations because they consent to the continuation of the political community by inheriting and enjoying property within that community. As we shall see, the strength of this argument depends upon the persuasiveness of Locke's doctrine of consent.

Locke also provides an argument against secession for the first generations of contractors on the grounds that the rationality of political society provides a strong reason not to secede, and the problem that secession might be a response to is not best dealt with by the dissolution of political society, but rather only by the dissolution of government and its reconstitution. The main point is that although we might have a reason to withdraw our consent and rebel against a government, we will retain, even in those circumstances, a reason to form political societies. The argument against secession is therefore partly provided by Locke's adoption of a two-stage contract. The first stage creates political society and the second constitutes a government. By distinguishing the political society and its government, Locke can assert the persistent legitimacy of political society as a solution to the inconveniences of the State of Nature, while allowing that the rejection of government on the grounds of its acting illegitimately might still be justified. Secession is an unnecessary response to the later issue of government legitimacy. Locke's suspicion of secession and his hostility to re-drawing boundaries has persisted into modern political theory, where general justifications of the right to secession are rare, with at best an acknowledgement of a special right to secession in response to persistent unjust treatment. As Locke would argue that persistent injustice is grounds for dissolving and reconstituting a legitimate government, he does not allow any right to secession.

The second stage agreement and the role of majorities

The second stage of Locke's original contract is the most important in terms of his own theory, as this concerns the establishment of government. Government, with its legislative and executive powers, is the primary good provided by political or civil society, as it is through government that our rights are protected and secured and the public good is promoted. By the public good is meant the provision of those things which maintain and enhance the system of rights and duties under law, such as the defence, security and judicial system, but it also means the provision of goods and services that are not implied by our particular rights, although not also precluded by them.

Where the establishment of political society involves the unanimous agreement of those who are members, the establishment of government only requires the agreement of a majority. Indeed in § 97 Locke argues:

> . . . every Man, by consenting with others to make one Body Politick under one Government, puts himself under an Obligation to every one of that Society, to submit to the determination of the *majority*, and to be concluded by it; or else this *original Compact*, whereby he with others incorporates into *one Society*, would signifie nothing, and be no Compact . . .

The idea of majority rule is found in other parts of Locke's argument; indeed it is used to justify the governance of women by men in the family. Yet the idea of majoritarian rule is often seen as in conflict with the rights-based arguments that Locke uses elsewhere in the *Second Treatise*. In contemporary liberal constitutionalism, rights are generally appealed to as a defence against majority rule, or the tyranny of the majority as J. S. Mill described it.[23] Libertarians such as Nozick see majoritarianism as the source of socialist redistributive policies that conflict with the absolute claim of rights. Yet Locke, who is one of the founders of modern liberalism and the inspiration of Nozick's libertarianism, appeals to majority judgement to decide the nature and structure of the government in his account of political society.

Are the commitment to basic rights and to majority decision-making compatible? In answering this question we need to be careful not to read too much into Locke's defence of majority decision-making. The first thing to note is that Locke does not appeal to the idea of a majority to decide the right answer in questions of fundamental morality. Majority decisions do not have a superior epistemic or normative status as a source of moral obligations. Locke is quite clear that in regard to our basic obligations under the Law of Nature, individual reason is the sole source of authoritative moral principles. Locke does not appeal to the judgement of a majority to settle any question of fundamental right. In this way his argument is very different from that of Rousseau's General Will. Instead, Locke introduces the idea of majority decision to settle the structure of the constitution of the state. As we shall see in a subsequent section he did not think that there was a unique constitutional structure to the state. In this case the constitution is an indifferent matter in that it is constrained and limited by the Law of Nature, but its details are not directly prescribed by an appeal to the fundamental law. People can legitimately differ about how to structure the constitution, how to order the ministries that make up the executive branch and how to settle the structure and frequency of meetings of the legislative. There is in effect no right answer to these questions and it is this problem that Locke wishes to solve by appealing to the will of the majority.

As Locke notes, deliberation on the nature and structure of government could be potentially endless if we sought a unanimous acceptance and this would undermine the point of the original agreement to form a state. In agreeing to leave the State of Nature we are in effect agreeing to limit our disagreement, which was after all the source of the major inconvenience of the pre-political condition. We should note here that in opting for a majority judgement Locke is conceding that political decision-making is different from fundamental moral deliberation and proceeds on the basis of feasibility rather than right. The second level of the original contract is not just the second part of the establishment of the state; it is effectively a separate sphere of decision-making with different criteria and standards.

But why should we adopt a majority decision rule? Locke has a number of responses to this question. The first and most important is that the majority judgement will tend to be the most legitimate because most people will actually endorse it and this is precisely the problem with the individual rule of an arbitrary monarch. Those who do not directly endorse a decision might, however, be said to consent to that majority decision by partaking in the decision-making process. This kind of argument is widely used in defences of majoritarianism in democratic decision-making. They claim that if one accepts the procedure for decision-making, one must accept the legitimacy of the outcome even if one is in the majority, just as in playing a game by the rules one must accept that one might not win.

This argument depends upon both procedural fairness and the absence of structural minorities who will always lose. Yet against this problem of structural minorities, we should note that Locke has already made membership of a political community a matter of unanimous consent, and therefore he is unlikely to face the problem of minority national communities in some modern states who are always effectively second-class citizens. The other important aspect to note is that he is appealing to the majority to decide the fundamental constitutional structure of the state, and although this will no doubt also include majority decision-making in the legislative, he does not think that the legislative should be particularly active.

The important point, however, remains that majorities indicate the effective power of the body of the political society in a way that individual judgements do not, and it is this ability to sway the body politic and make it act effectively that concerns Locke most. It is precisely this kind of argument that Locke appeals to in justifying the rule of the strongest or most physically powerful in the family. The harnessing of effective power to protect and secure our most basic rights is precisely what we seek in leaving the State of Nature, for it is that which the Law of Nature lacks. Locke's argument does indeed seem to be that there is safety in numbers. We should, however, note that the harnessing of majority power is to protect and secure our rights, so although Locke does acknowledge the importance of considerations of power in political theory he still subordinates the claims of power, even majority power, to the claims of right.

The problem of consent

The concept of consent is used throughout the *Second Treatise* to distinguish legitimate from illegitimate political power and remains one of the most distinctive aspects of Locke's contribution to the social contract tradition, yet he does not really examine the idea until relatively late on in the book at § 119. In this famous passage Locke distinguishes between express and tacit versions of consent.

> No body doubts but an *express Consent*, of any Man, entring into any Society, makes him a perfect Member of that Society, a Subject of that Government. The difficulty is, what ought to be look'd upon as a *tacit Consent*, and how far it binds, *i.e.* how far any one shall be looked on to have consented, and thereby submitted to any Government, where he has made no Expressions

of it at all. And to this I say, that every Man, that hath any Possession, or Enjoyment, or any part of the Dominions of any Government, doth thereby give his *tacit Consent*, and is as far forth obliged to Obedience to the Laws of that Government, during such Enjoyment, as any one under it; whether this his Possession be of Land, to him and his Heirs for ever, or a Lodging only for a Week; or whether it be barely travelling freely on the Highway; (§ 119)

Express consent is straightforward and involves explicit agreements such as promises and oaths of allegiance whereby individuals consciously place themselves under clear obligations. But of course not all individuals take such oaths, and in Locke's day very few Englishmen could be said to have expressly consented, so this provided at best only a partial account of legitimacy and political obligation. Furthermore, Locke was aware that an original contract to establish a civil society would at best bind the original contractors and therefore leave all future generations without an obligation to obey the state, or worse still, given the challenge of political absolutism, subject to alternative accounts of political obligation that made no reference to consent. To overcome this problem Locke introduced the idea of tacit consent, an idea that we have already encountered in the account of the invention of money in Chapter V of the *Second Treatise*. In this section I want to examine what Locke means by consent and whether tacit consent is really a form of consent at all.

We use the concept of consent in everyday life and it forms an important part of our legal discourse, but it remains a complicated and elusive concept. When we use the concept we tend to imply a number of things, the first of which is a background condition of freedom. To consent to an act we need to be free to do or refrain from doing that act. As we shall see later in the discussion of conquest, Locke rejects the idea of consent at the point of a sword that we find in Hobbes' contract theory. For Locke such consent is simply a version of coercion and no source of obligation. Instead we must genuinely be able to act otherwise and where the costs of acting are not so great as to make a choice untenable. Thus it is not good enough to say that the woman forced to consent to sex at knife-point by a rapist is actually consenting to her assault, nor will it do to say that a person consents to hand over their wallet to a highwayman, simply because in both cases the victim could have chosen death. Yet while Locke's rejection of the Hobbesian approach is intuitively appealing and matches our considered use of the concept in legal and moral discourse, it is still subject to a number of problems. Locke's ideal of free consent leaves us with the necessity of identifying genuinely free choices. As we have seen this is not simply a matter of listing alternatives, as both the rape and robbery victim have an alternative option – death! We might respond that the options need to be realistic, but that raises a number of complex philosophical questions about the nature of free choice, including the most problematic question, namely whether we are ever genuinely free to do anything. I will not pursue the fundamental question of freedom of the will in Locke's philosophy, not least because he avoids discussion of the matter in the *Second Treatise*, but the problem does remain in the background of his theory, not least because Locke does employ a normative conception of freedom in the State of Nature that is contrasted with mere licence, or pure negative liberty of the kind just noted in Hobbes. As this is the case, we must note that for Locke we cannot consent to acts that are outside the Law of Nature even if we think we can. We cannot, for example, consent to our own slavery, nor can we consent to our own death, despite the claims of some philosophers in contemporary debates about assisted suicide involving the terminally ill, and the fact that many people today do not have a problem with the idea of freely consenting to one's own death.

We should also note that Locke's view of the freedom constraint underlying consent does not seem to acknowledge sources of social or conventional coercion. As we saw in the case of the status of women in the family, the tyranny of patriarchal conventions does not undermine, for Locke, the idea that women do tacitly consent to their domestic subordination and governance. Neither does Locke see any coercion in the tacit consent to the introduction of inequality that follows from the invention and adoption of money.

Alongside the background condition of freedom we can also identify three further conditions of free consent.[24] These are that in order for consent to be genuine a person must

1. know what she consents to;
2. intend to consent;
3. be able to communicate the consent and the intention to consent.

In the case of express consent, a person can satisfy the first condition by answering a question such as expressing a vow in a marriage ceremony. The response reminds the person of what it is they are agreeing to. Similarly taking an oath of office involves acknowledging a series of obligations that are usually stated in the oath. In each case, as long as the consenter can read and understand the oath or vow, they can be assumed to satisfy the knowledge condition. Those who lack the intellectual capacity cannot be assumed to satisfy this condition and it is for this reason that Locke excludes children from his consent-based account of political obligations. We also tend to accept this condition on children by placing a minimum age for marriage and inheritance contracts and sexual consent. Yet even in the case of express consent we might argue that the knowledge condition is not as straightforward as it seems. How much of an understanding can we assume an ordinary person to have of the full implications of their agreement?

In the case of the intention to consent, the examples of oaths, promises and agreements require a specific act in an institutional context which usually precludes any mistaken act of consent. Once a person can at least understand where they are and what people are saying to them, the institutional setting of a marriage contract, oath of allegiance or office, will indicate the intention of the agent in the absence of external conditions such as angry fathers with shotguns, or troops threatening a recently conquered population. Similar considerations apply in the case of the communication of consent. Promises, vows and oaths are performative utterances that only work in a particular institutional setting. They also require some verbalization as a sign of communicating agreement. In the case of taking an oath of office or exchanging a marriage vow, it is not enough to nod or smile; the agent concerned must repeat a form of words.

Having explored these simple conditions of free consent and seen how the idea of express consent can satisfy them, we need to turn to the more problematic idea of tacit consent, both in the famous § 119 and in the other places where the idea is used in the *Second Treatise*. In the quotation given above, Locke explicitly states that tacit consent is given by enjoying possession of land but also enjoying merely the protection of the laws when one walks along the highway, or even being in a country. David Hume had much fun with this last claim in his famous essay 'Of the Original Contract' where he writes:

Can we seriously say that a poor peasant or artisan has a free choice to leave his country when he knows no foreign language or manners and lives from day to day by the small wages which he acquires? We may as well assert that a man, by remaining in a vessel, freely consents to the dominion of the master, though he was carried on board while asleep and must leap into the ocean and perish the moment he leaves her.[25]

We can see in Hume's quick dismissal of the argument that tacit consent is indeed a version of consent, that the idea has some problems. If we start with the knowledge constraint we can see that it is difficult to make sense of this in the case of tacit consent. None of the actions, with the exception of the inheritance of property, involves a single institutional dimension, so there is no obvious signal to the actor that what they are doing has precisely the implications that Locke claims. Perhaps one could get around this by widely promulgating the idea that all of the general actions that Locke alludes to constitute forms of consent and agreement with political rule. This would require a more extensive and intrusive state than Locke wants, but it might be one way in which the knowledge condition could be satisfied. However, if we take a specific example of tacit consent within Locke's argument, namely the consent to inequality that follows from the acceptance of money, we might argue that the knowledge condition is problematic. Locke's claim is that in accepting money we consent to the inequalities that follow from it but is this a reasonable claim? Could one in a primitive state of the sort Locke envisages have any understanding of the nature and scope of inequalities that an advanced economy makes possible? The sort of difference between richest and poorest in Locke's time, though considerable, would be insignificant compared to the inequalities that are possible in our own advanced economies. The point is not whether these inequalities might not be justified in some other way, it is simply whether it makes sense to claim that people, at the time the convention of money use was established, could have comprehended the huge inequalities that might have existed between the likes of Bill Gates and a casual fruit picker.

If the knowledge condition is difficult to satisfy in the case of tacit consent, a bigger problem is posed by the intention and the communication conditions. In the case of enjoying the protection of the laws or travelling on the highway, it is hard to envisage how one might signify the intention NOT to consent. After all, trying to flee the state would itself involve travelling the highway and consequently would seem to indicate tacit consent, even if those fleeing intend no such thing. If one cannot in principle signify non-consent, then almost every action will count as a species of consent and therefore the idea becomes meaningless and redundant. In this way the idea of tacit consent fails both the intentionality condition and the communication condition, as there is no possibility of expressing the absence of consent which is not at the same time an example of consenting, and every act one engages in, even acts of resistance, would appear to communicate some form of consent. If we turn again to the apparent tacit consent to inequality that follows from the adoption of money, it is again unclear how the acceptance of money could indicate an intention to accept inconceivable inequalities, and how this intention could be communicated. How could one for example reject gross inequalities but accept limited ones? Alternatively, could one accept the use of money as a medium of exchange without being said to consent to all the advantages that go with monopoly power in a situation of imperfect competition? It is not even clear that in accepting primitive currency one is faced with an option of separating out the various things that one might wish to consent to, if one could even understand them.

In the end the idea of tacit consent is incoherent and runs contrary to much of Locke's argument about the importance of consent. One charitable response to these criticisms is to narrow down the scope of Locke's account of tacit consent to core cases of accepting the implications of certain legally constituted benefits such as property in land or capital. Here Locke's argument seems more like an example of express consent, where inheritance brings with it the assumption of certain obligations as well as rights, and the enjoyment of these might be said to reasonably entail the endorsement of the system that makes them possible. In this way the act of inheritance might prove a much less problematic example of tacit consent. The enjoyment of property, whether by a resident or an alien engaged in trade, and by implication the enjoyment of the laws that protect it, is the core case of tacit consent in § 119. If we read the rest of the brief passage as an extension of the enjoyment of the protection of private property under the law, then it is possible to identify a more tenable conception of tacit consent in this passage. This narrower reading salvages the idea of tacit consent, but at a cost. If the idea is now more closely attached to the idea of the enjoyment of private property, then potentially we are back with the exclusion of most individuals from political obligation on the ground of their having no property. Perhaps one might argue that everybody has some property in their labour and their ability to earn wages. But even this reading, which places less emphasis on real property in land, would still exclude the unemployed from political obligation, but it would also extend the idea of tacit consent back in the all-encompassing direction of the literal reading of the passage from § 119 with all of the problems we have just discussed.

Although the account of tacit consent fails to provide a general account of political obligation for those who are not involved in the original establishment of political society, or who do not expressly consent to it through oaths of allegiance, it remains of interest as it points to two alternative approaches to the problem of political obligation. In the general account of tacit consent in § 119 there are also intimations of a utilitarian account and a fairness account of political obligation. Neither of these is developed in Locke's *Second Treatise*, although it is fair to say that Locke does seem to oscillate between a strict consent view and a justice view of legitimacy, the latter of which would follow from these accounts.

A utilitarian theory of political obligation claims that we have an obligation to obey the state when the state and its institutions promote the maximum utility or welfare of the subject population. This is the sort of argument that David Hume and Jeremy Bentham make later in the eighteenth century. Both thinkers refer to the kinds of benefits provided by the Lockean state, but they separate these from their origin in a contract or act of consent. Indeed both argue that it is the recognition of the potential benefits that would give us a reason for consenting in the first instance, so providing a sufficient reason for political obligation and showing the redundancy of the idea of consent. The benefit of this kind of argument is that it does not depend on showing some form of act of consent that everybody in the state must make. This saves the utilitarian from the contortions of Locke's theory of tacit consent, but at the same time it provides a general obligation of the sort that Locke appears to want. If we look at the list of benefits, the enjoyment of which is supposed to signify tacit consent, we can argue that these benefits on their own are a significant source of utility or welfare and therefore a basis for a generalized obligation to obey the state. Fundamental goods, such as the enjoyment of property, the ability to travel freely on the highway and the security that allows people to go about their business, are precisely the kinds of benefits that utilitarians appeal to. Locke does appeal to utilitarian considerations towards the end of the *Second Treatise* when he considers how an individual should respond to a violation of their rights that does not indicate a general dissolution of government. So the argument from utility is not wholly alien to Locke's theory.

Yet utilitarian arguments are not without their own difficulties, as they make the idea of obligation conditional upon the enjoyment of a level of benefits that are generally advantageous, yet for any particular individual at any particular time they may be burdensome and contrary to one's immediate welfare. Compliance with the laws of property might well be in the general interest over the long run, but if an alternative distribution of property was even more beneficial then we clearly have a reason to change the system of property and institute a new one, even if the government of the day is not acting beyond its constitutional powers. Both Hume and Bentham were concerned about this radical potential of utilitarian arguments.

More troubling still for Locke is the possibility of an illiberal state still providing some of the benefits of civility and order and therefore satisfying the conditions of a utilitarian justification. Very few governments are wholly arbitrary in their actions, so even some of the worst regimes in modern history might satisfy some minimally utilitarian account of political obligation. After all, even in Nazi Germany people bought and sold property, entered into commercial contracts and had the criminal law enforced against ordinary burglars and thieves, whatever else the state might have been doing against the Jewish population. Similarly, in Locke's day the rule of Charles II and then James II was not without the continued enforcement of much of the law. Many conservatives of Locke's own day would have used some version of these utilitarian arguments to support the claim for political obligation to the Stuart Crown.

The second argument we find intimated in Locke's account of tacit consent is the argument from fairness, which has become an important account of political obligation in recent political philosophy. Just as with tacit consent and utilitarian arguments, the fairness argument relies on the benefits of social cooperation. The difference is that it uses this idea of the general benefits of social cooperation to justify an obligation to accept one's fair share of the burdens of social and political cooperation, such as obeying the law when it is not immediately to one's advantage, or paying one's taxes. Admittedly, very little of this fairness argument can be derived from the passage in § 119, other than the list of potential benefits of social cooperation, but we can see something like this argument underlying the role of trust and discretion in Locke's account of political rule, where Locke argues that we must accept an obligation to the government of the state even if we disagree with how the Executive power of the state is used, subject to the constraint of that use being within the bounds of the Law of Nature. The advantage of the fairness argument over the utilitarian argument in light of Locke's concerns is that the former involves us in far less by way of compromises with arbitrary regimes that violate rights. The argument from fairness places far more by way of constraints on what the state can legitimately do. Although Locke does not develop either the utilitarian or fairness argument, it is certainly interesting to note in closing this discussion that he was aware of the problematic character of his own consent-based account of a general obligation to obey the state and intimated the directions in which subsequent accounts of political obligation would develop.

vi THE LOCKEAN STATE

Having provided an account of the origin of political society and the theory of express and tacit consent, Locke provides a brief theory of the state in §§ 123–69. His account concentrates on a number of normative problems about the limitation of government power rather than a fully worked out account of the structure of the state and its various functions. This reticence is partly because Locke was a libertarian who believed that the less legislative government there was the better, as it tended to overstep its competence if it met and acted too frequently (§ 156), but it was also because Locke conceded that history and varied circumstances shaped the different forms of constitution such that little is gained by trying to set out all the various ministries and functions in a work of political philosophy (§ 152). Although many subsequent political theorists such as Montesquieu (1689–1755) and Bentham spent much time drafting ideal constitutions or explaining the various tasks of government, much political philosophy since Locke has abandoned the task providing an ideal constitution as this was technical work more properly done by those with practical legal expertise. Indeed in the case of Jeremy Bentham, writing just over a century after Locke's *Second Treatise*, many have argued that he gave up political philosophy for a more empirically oriented political science. Although political philosophy can add little to the task of designing government ministries and functions, Locke still thought that it had an important justificatory role to play. His concern is not with the practical competence of branches of government but more with the normative legitimacy of branches of government. He provides little by way of an account of the detailed structure of constitutional government but he does still add something to our understanding of the basic principles which underlay it.

A further familiar feature of Locke's argument is the way that he uses the account of legislative supremacy and the account of the limitation on executive and prerogative power to challenge some of the prevailing absolutist prejudices of his day. We will look at these issues shortly, although relatively briefly, as Locke's theory of the state is less central to the main argument of the *Second Treatise* than his account of the right of private property or the theory of consent.

In § 133 Locke explains that he uses the word commonwealth to indicate an independent community or what the Romans referred to as a *Civitas*. What he is suggesting to us is that his concern is with a distinctly political community that cannot be identified with a place or function such as a city or a guild. Locke is referring to the peculiarly political form of community that we now refer to as a state as distinct from a country or a nation. The types of commonwealth all vary according to Locke in terms of who exercises legislative power. If it is exercised by one man we tend to refer to it as a monarchy, if on the other hand it is exercised by a number of men we describe it as an oligarchy. Again we might distinguish types of monarchy in terms of how the person who currently exercises legislative power is chosen. If he is chosen by birth then the monarchy is hereditary and if by election then we might refer to an elective monarchy. Perhaps Locke is suggesting to his contemporaries that they might choose their next monarch?

Yet beyond this brief discussion Locke has very little to say about the forms of government, unlike his classical forbears such as Aristotle who devoted much attention to examining different kinds of constitution, at least until Locke returns to the brief discussion of corrupt constitutions that forms part of his defence of the right to resist and rebel. We might wonder why Locke, who was a great advocate of empirical science, was not more concerned like Aristotle with the types of constitution. The simple answer is not that Locke was a crude rationalist who was preoccupied by a theory; rather it is that Locke has a clearer sense of the intellectual division of labour between philosophy, science and history. In Chapter XII Locke distinguishes three main functions within the constitution of a commonwealth, these are the Legislative, the Executive and the Federative. Locke had already begun explaining the nature of Legislative power in Chapter XI but it is appropriate to jump ahead a little to examine this classification. Modern constitutionalism enshrined in the example of Constitution of the United States of America provides a tripartite division of powers into Legislative, Executive and Judiciary. The concern of the American Founders was to separate and balance powers within the Constitution so that each would check the other and thus limit arbitrary and corrupt rule. The whole point was to make the exercise of political power difficult so that its abuse would also be difficult. Locke's concern in the *Second Treatise* is different in that he is not offering a theory of how a constitution should be constructed if one wishes to achieve certain political ends. Instead he provides an account of the primary functions of government. Legislation and the Executive power of government is relatively straightforward. The Legislative is the power of making laws and the Executive is that power of government which enforces the law. For Locke the Executive will include the Judiciary as a permanent part of the enforcement of law. What is curious is his distinction of the third function or the Federative power. He describes the Federative as the power of making treaties, entering leagues and alliances and going to war (§§ 145–7). Ordinarily we would see this as a necessary part of the power of the Executive. In the United Kingdom the prime minister still exercises the right to go to war as part of the Royal Prerogative and in the United States the power to go to war can be located in either the Legislature or the Executive, with the former conferring the power on the latter as Commander-in-Chief of the armed forces. In neither case do we seem to have a need for a further power or function. Why does Locke distinguish the Executive and the Federative? The reason is subtle and concerns the nature of the power and not who exercises it. As Locke goes on to acknowledge in § 148, both powers can be exercised by the same person; indeed they must be exercised by the same person, because if they were exercised by different persons we would in effect have two sovereigns who could conflict and this would cause internal chaos. The more important point concerns the nature of the powers themselves. The Executive power concerns the domestic enforcement of the law and is therefore a power that is defined by the fundamental law of the state and limited by that power. The Federative power on the other hand concerns a realm in which there is no agreed constitutional framework as each state is effectively in a State of Nature with each other. The Federative power is bound by the Law of Nature but only in the same way as the power of individuals is bound by the Law of Nature prior to political society. The two powers are fundamentally different in their scope and in the respective judgements that have to be made by the institutions of government. Within the Constitution the Executive power is largely constrained by the Legislative (although not wholly as we shall see), whereas the Federative power is a power of much less restricted judgement. As Locke says,

> . . . though this *federative Power* in the well or ill management of it be of great moment to the commonwealth, yet it is much less capable to be directed by antecedent, standing, positive Laws, than the *Executive*; and so must be left to the Prudence and Wisdom of those whose hands it is in, to be managed for the publick good. (§ 147)

Legislative power

Of the three types of power found in the Commonwealth the most important is the Legislative. This Locke calls the supreme power, at least until government is dissolved when the supreme power reverts to the people who may reconstitute the government as they wish. This gives some clue as to why the Legislative is the supreme power. It is that power which is constituted by the people through their consent to become a particular political society with a common authority to regulate their respective claims and to enforce and secure their rights. As ultimate political power is solely based upon consent of the governed and this is expressed through the Legislative power of the State, there cannot by definition be a higher political power than Legislative power. Legislative power is the sanctioned will of the political community, but it is subject to four main conditions which place limits upon what can count as legitimate laws. Once again, we can see that Locke rejects the simple absolutist account of legislation in terms of the origin of Legislative authority in the will of a sovereign individual or body. For Locke, sovereign Legislative power must also satisfy some substantive conditions of legitimacy, otherwise it ceases to be law and we are therefore under no obligation to obey it. These conditions are:

1. Legislative power cannot be arbitrarily exercised over the people. Law is restricted to the protection of the civil interests of the people – their lives, liberties and property – and all this for the common good. It is only to secure the protection of these things that people unite themselves together as a commonwealth. To seek to use the law to do more than protect the rights and civil interests of men would therefore conflict with the eternal rule of the Law of Nature which remains the ultimate criterion of legitimacy.

2. As such it must be exercised through clear and determinate laws and enforced by independent and known judges. It is the rule of law and not of men. Locke's point here is similar to the claim he made about the Law of Nature being something accessible to all independent of special revelation. Nobody can be bound by a law that they could not know or comprehend. As political power will involve the codification and regulation of the claims of the Law of Nature which may provide the basis for disputes, it needs to be set down in clear positive laws that are publicly promulgated and fairly applied.

3. No one can be deprived of her property without consent. So there can be no taxation without consent and representation. Given that no one can be unlawfully deprived of their life or their liberty either, it is not clear why Locke singles out the restriction on expropriation as a criterion of legitimate power other than to reinforce the idea that private property is a pre-political right that is not created and therefore revocable by the Legislative power.

4. Finally the legislature cannot transfer the power of making laws to another body – such as another state or a religious authority. French kings or Catholic popes cannot make English laws and it is only by the express will of the English people that they recognize any government as lawful. In transferring law-making

power to another sovereign, the legislature effectively dissolves itself and therefore ceases to be a Legislative power. That said, the people could submit to another king (such as William III) but it would only be through their free and express consent that this happened and not by an act of legislation. Once again, Locke is perhaps reminding Parliament that only the consent of the people can transfer the Crown and the right to make laws – a lesson that is as applicable to the case of the Protestant William III as the Catholic James II.

Executive power

The supreme power in the state is the Legislative power and it is this that Locke discusses most extensively, yet he points out that the Legislative power should not be assembled and exercised too frequently as this tends to corruption, and nor is it necessary that it should sit constantly. Locke has a minimal view of government, very unlike the modern welfare or bureaucratic state, where the task of legislation and regulation seems to be constant. Even our contemporary politicians who claim to be following the spirit of Locke's minimal state still tend to find much Legislative and regulatory work to do even under the guise of shrinking the state and cutting expenditure.

Locke clearly thought that the Legislative assembly should sit infrequently and be called into action only when pressing business demanded it. Unlike eighteenth- and nineteenth-century reformers who called for frequent and regular parliaments (even annual parliaments), Locke suggests that the power to convene Parliament should be vested in the Executive or that part of the government which continues to function when the Legislative is not sitting.

As we have seen, Locke does not have much to say about the internal organization of Executive power and whether it should be vested in one man or many and how the various ministries should be structured. No general account can be given of the internal structure of the Executive branch. Instead Locke focuses his attention on the relationship between the Legislative and the Executive branches of government. His primary concern is not to specify how Executive power should be organized but rather to explain how it is that the Executive – in the person of the English monarchy – came to claim priority over the Legislative which was located in Parliament. The discussion is not historical but is philosophical, and it is designed to show how it was possible to confuse the respective claims of both branches. This confusion led to the claims for the supremacy of the king over Parliament.

As we have seen, Locke defines the supremacy of the Legislative branch on the grounds that it is the expressed will of the political community providing laws for itself. The Executive branch is subordinate in that its task is to enforce the laws provided by the Legislative branch. While government remains in place and acts within its powers there cannot be a power superior to the Legislative. How then did we arrive at a claim for the priority of Executive power? One reason is that the Executive branch is permanently in place whereas the Legislative meets only occasionally. But the more important reason for the confusion is that the power to call the Legislative is a trust exercised by the Executive. It is because the Executive alone has the power to convene the Legislative assembly that it might appear to have a supremacy over the Legislative branch, but this would be a misunderstanding. There is the appearance of supremacy, but Locke is clear to point out that this is really only an appearance, as the Executive does not have a will or power other than that granted to it by the Legislative. The Executive merely executes a legally constituted function, albeit one that is very important. The function is, however, the exercise of a trust and not the sort of mechanical function that is involved in calling elections today in modern constitutional democracies. Even in Britain, where the prime minister has some discretion over when to call an election, he must still call one within a five-year period. In other mature democracies, such as that of the US, the Executive term is set out in law and the President cannot serve more than two four-year terms. For Locke, the Executive branch must exercise its judgement when it is necessary to reconvene the Legislative assembly, and given that Locke thought there should not be too much Legislative activity, he did not think it possible to lay down how frequently the assembly should sit.

There remains one important problem that arises from entrusting the power to convene the Legislative assembly to the Executive branch, and that concerns what happens when the Executive refuses to convene the assembly. This was a serious matter for Locke, as it was a familiar strategy of Charles II to refuse to call parliaments into session for fear that they would try and limit his powers or cut off funding. In such cases, Locke's defence of Executive discretion seems to allow the Executive branch to refuse to call the assembly into being. Locke's solution to this problem prefigures his account of the right to rebel, which we will examine later. The refusal to call the Legislative into assembly when there is a public need is a violation of the trust exercised within the constitution and therefore an act of aggression against the people which they are entitled to defend themselves against. If the refusal to assemble the Legislative results in a threat to the people's civil interests or the public good then it is clearly a breach of the Law of Nature. As we shall see, the problem of when the trust is breached is not easy to determine and Locke does not provide a simple rule for deciding when this happens. His assumption is that the potential threat requiring a Legislative response will be public, obvious and pressing so that the refusal to convene the assembly will appear a clear breach of trust. Yet there are no doubt many cases where a refusal to call the Legislative appears a clear breach to some and yet to others it will seem an equally clear and legitimate exercise of Executive discretion. Locke does not provide a clear answer to this problem.

The final problem that Locke addresses in his discussion of the Executive branch concerns the character and reform of the Legislative assembly. Here his concern is with the structure of representation. Legislative assemblies represent groups of people in elective constituencies. Yet the character of these constituencies can change over long periods of time. Constituencies that were once thriving can end up with very few residents as people move and populations change. When this happens the ideal of equal representation is threatened. Locke clearly has in mind the idea of rotten and pocket boroughs in England that very often had few if any electors and yet were still able to return members to the Legislative. This problem was to become a matter of considerable concern among political radicals throughout the eighteenth century. It was not until the nineteenth century that parliamentary reform was achieved. Locke is clearly acknowledging a problem that would be taken up by subsequent radicals. His commitment to the ideal of equal representation (§ 158) is also an important indication that despite his liberal suspicion of government he was by no means a conservative when it came to issues of political representation. Indeed he sees the only solution to the problem of Legislative reform in the hands of the Executive, as the Legislative assembly has an institutional interest in maintaining the status quo. But if the Executive can change the electoral map, then again it would seem that it has a supreme power to alter the terms of the constitution, despite Locke's clear assertion that only the people can alter the terms of the constitution once the government has dissolved itself. Locke's answer to the problem is to deny that the Executive would be altering the constitution. Instead, he claims that the Executive in this case would be perfectly within its constitutional power of enforcing the law under the constitution by returning to the original constitutional commitment to equal representation. Such an action would reform the original constitution rather than form a radical departure from it and as such it would be within the spirit of the constitution.

Prerogative

The account of Executive power includes an acknowledgement of prerogative power which also involves, as we have just seen, the power to reform the electoral system of the Legislative assembly. Locke's brief discussion of prerogative power is designed to defend its compatibility with the rule of law and constitutional government, but also to explain why the idea has given rise to a unique set of powers exercised by a monarch beyond the control of the Legislative or the people. Locke wants to defend the first sense of prerogative but to deny the second.

Prerogative power is essentially the power to act to mitigate the unforeseen and harmful consequences of a strict adherence to the rule of law. In § 159 Locke gives two clear examples of the use of prerogative power. The first concerns the power to pull down buildings in order to prevent the spread of fire and the second concerns the power to mitigate the severity of a sentence when this does no harm to the innocent. In the first case Locke is actually suggesting that the Executive can interfere with the rights of private property. This would seem to contradict one of his conditions of legitimacy which provides for an absolute defence of the right to private property. Yet Locke's point is that the system of private property cannot be enforced in a way that allows for widespread harm to the property rights of others. So in the event of a densely populated neighbourhood being subject to a fire, it is to prevent harm to the property rights of the majority that the Executive may pull down the property of adjacent buildings to prevent the spread of the fire.

The justification of the exercise of prerogative power must be the prevention of harm that would result from the strict application of the law, and where that harm would be to the system of rights. Yet this does not entail arbitrary rule as there is no prerogative right to act contrary to the Law of Nature. As men are rational, Locke claims, they could not have conferred on the Executive a prerogative power that precisely threatened those things that men entered civil society to protect. This rationality test is then supposed to help us distinguish cases of legitimate prerogative from arbitrary and lawless power. Once again what falls within the legitimate prerogative of the Executive will be a matter of judgement, but it cannot include many of the claims to unaccountable power that were made by monarchical absolutists. The absolutists claim that prerogative is a species of political power that is not conditional on the consent of the people and is beyond the legitimate scrutiny of the Legislative branch of government. Locke clearly denies that such power is legitimate but he also wants to explain how this form of apparent prerogative arose. He does this by referring to the earliest forms of government when there would have been very little by way of positive law and therefore considerable discretion on the part of the Executive power as to how these laws should be applied. The idea of monarchical prerogative arises when this discretion is exercised wisely and in the public good. In such circumstances this exercise of power does not attract the hostility of the people and it is borne with equanimity. As long as the monarch is striving for the public good there is no problem and often there is very little reason to object. The problem arises when this exercise of discretionary power is used as a precedent by later monarchs who do not necessarily act in accordance with the public good. Because the exercise of power has been tolerated over time, it is seen to be a legitimate and unaccountable power of the monarch even when it is no longer exercised wisely or for the public good. Locke's point is to show how the idea of the Royal prerogative might arise, but he is clear to reject the idea that this historical precedent creates any claim to legitimacy. Prerogative and Executive discretion must ultimately be tested against the standard of reason and the public good. If they fail this test they are illegitimate and can be resisted as one would resist any other assault from an unjust aggressor. This brings us to the most controversial aspect of Locke's argument: his defence of the right to rebel.

vii CONQUEST, TYRANNY AND THE DISSOLUTION OF THE STATE

The remaining five chapters of Locke's *Second Treatise* (§§ 169–243) are among the most controversial of the whole book. In one sense they merely tie up some loose ends and draw some simple conclusions from the preceding account of the nature and limits of a constitutionally limited state and the appropriate understanding of political power and authority. Just as the great political philosophers from Plato and Aristotle onwards have provided accounts of the corrupt forms of government, so Locke also provides a discussion of the ways in which governments can become despotical or tyrannical. But unlike these earlier philosophers, Locke does not provide an analysis of the structure of corrupt forms of the state or the character of corrupt rulers. Instead he focuses on the ways any regime whether monarchical, aristocratic or popular can cease to be legitimate by breaching trust with the governed or by illegitimately acquiring power.

Yet alongside this focus on legitimacy and illegitimacy of political rule these final five chapters spell out a right of rebellion against illegitimate political rule, which in some respects was Locke's manifesto for the removal of the Stuart monarchs and warning to their successors William and Mary, that their power was to be exercised as a trust at the pleasure of the people. For many commentators on Locke since his own times, everything that has gone before in the *Second Treatise* is merely a prelude to the argument for a right to rebellion, in response to those absolutists such as Hobbes who argued that the benefits of any form of political rule, no matter how tyrannical (and he claimed one man's tyrant was merely another man's strong ruler), was always better than the costs and pains of civil war and chaos. Other absolutists such as Filmer tended to argue that rebellion was an assault on the divinely sanctioned natural order and therefore a crime against God and Nature. Each of these arguments tend to retain a consequentialist critique of civil war and rebellion. If these consequentialist arguments are allowed to stand then no amount of government oppression or cruelty will warrant the immeasurably greater harm done by the threat of rebellion. Political conservatives will always be able to use the threat of the greater chaos posed by any challenge to the status quo in order to excuse any amount of arbitrary or even despotical rule. Locke saw this kind of argument as a 'slippery slope' that could lead to any kind of despotical rule, including in his own day the imposition of an alien religion such as Catholicism and the denial of civil and political liberties, all in the name of security. The argument that security and political stability, however achieved, must have priority over any other value or end is not unfamiliar in our own contemporary politics. It can be found in *ex post facto* defences of cruel authoritarian regimes such as that of Saddam Hussein, where it is suggested that however bad his regime was it was better than the chaos unleashed by his removal. Similarly, the argument is used by those who seek ever greater curtailments of civil and political liberties in the face of a threat to national security.

Locke's conclusion is intensely political as he turns attention from the analysis of legitimate political power to political advocacy and a challenge to the prevalence of consequentialist defences of political subjection. In the end, Locke wants to defend the idea that there are both worse things than civil disorder and that sometimes the threat of civil disorder and rebellion is not only legitimate but also a desirable trump card to hold political power within legitimate constraints.

This final section of the book begins at Chapter XV with a brief restatement of Locke's distinction between political, paternal and despotical power. The point is to distinguish each from the other and explain their origins as Locke thought that considerable mischief resulted from their confusion. Political power as we have seen is the right of making laws with penalties of death and all other penalties for the purpose of protecting property and the good of the community (see § 3); this form of power is derived only from the voluntary consent of those subject to it. This is distinguishable from paternal power, which does not include a right to impose penalties up to and including death, as parents are not allowed to kill their children, even though children are not full moral equals with rights. Paternal or parental power is derived from nature, but only extends to the right of tuition of a child and not to their person, liberty or possessions. Despotical power does include the right to kill, but crucially for Locke it only arises in the rare circumstances of a deferred punishment of an aggressor taken in a just war. Despotical power over a person can therefore only be legitimate where that person has forfeited his or her Natural Rights by attacking or threatening force against another person. This suggests that Locke does think that despotical power can in some circumstances be legitimate, but his main point is that we should not confuse despotical rule with political rule, for if we do we must accept that we are slaves whose lives are enjoyed only at the pleasure of our ruler. If this is what the absolutist wants to claim then they should do so clearly and openly. If they do, they are unlikely to find many who agree that political authority should be exercised in the same way that a despot treats his slaves. This distinction between political rule and despotical rule is complicated by the fact of conquest as this shows both that many states are not based on consent and that on the basis of conquest many subjects do indeed appear to be in the situation of slaves. Let us turn first to Locke's discussion of conquest.

Conquest

Conquest is an interesting and pressing issue for Locke to consider, for the following reason. Hobbes famously used conquest to provide his second account of sovereignty. Here the idea is that most (if not all) states are not based on primordial agreements but rather on conquest, yet that that does not matter because conquest is a legitimate source of political power as it is a form of contract. Hobbes is able to make this claim because he argues that binding agreements can be made under duress or at the 'point of a sword'. If this is so then if a conqueror offers us our lives in return for subjection, and if we choose our lives, we have agreed to our subjection. When we apply this to history we can see that force of arms such as William the Conqueror's successful defeat of the Anglo-Saxons in 1066 effectively places subsequent generations of Englishmen under the authority of William and his heirs. Hobbes' argument is particularly serious as it seems to combine the claims of abstract philosophical contractarianism with a sense of history. Once again, although we should not read Locke's argument as a simple response to Hobbes', we can see how the same issue underlies Locke's argument about conquest. But Locke's argument is also more subtly provocative in that it effectively denies that William of Orange's capture of the British Crown by force of arms creates a legitimate claim to rule. Again Locke can be seen as offering a subtle reminder to his former associates that political authority can only ever be based on consent voluntarily given. It cannot be won in battle or extracted at the point of a sword.

The argument against conquest as a source of government is simple. Locke reasserts that political societies can only be founded on the consent of the governed and that although history might seem to show that many states appear to arise from conquest and war, such that force of arms may be taken for consent of the people, this is a mistake. Conquest does not create states, it only destroys them and we should no more mistake it for creating legitimate political societies than we should mistake the demolition of a house for its construction (§ 175). If a conquest is the result of an unjust war then it creates no right at all, any more than a thief can obtain a right in another man's property by taking it by force. Might has no bearing on right, contrary to Hobbes' claim.

But not all conquests are the result of unjust wars. We can in our own time see the occupations of Germany and Japan following the Second World War as cases of conquest that results from a just war. What does Locke have to say about such cases? In this case it would seem that some form of despotical rule is legitimate. Locke's response to this challenge is to acknowledge the claim to despotical rule, but to qualify it so much as to deny the claim the force to support political despotism.

Locke argues that the conqueror by conquest in a just war gains no lawful right over those who are engaged in conquest with him. So in the case of William the Conqueror in 1066, his successful defeat of the Anglo-Saxons gives him a right of despotical rule over the defeated and captured army, but it gives him no such right over his companions the Norman barons who conquered with him. If they choose to acknowledge William as their king then his authority is based on, and limited by, consent; he cannot rule despotically over them. Similarly, he has an obligation to share the spoils of the just war with his companions who in so far as they are engaged only in the pursuit of a just war are allowed to recover the cost of the campaign and to recompense any loss that resulted in the war in the first instance.

With respect to those who are conquered, Locke claims that despotical rule only extends over those who were actually engaged in the unjust war. If we jump forward from the case of 1066 to 1945, Locke's claim would be that the victorious powers only have legitimate despotical authority over those who were engaged in prosecuting the unjust war. Civilians and non-combatants are not only immune in battle, but are not responsible for the unjust war, unless they consented to it, and participated in it. Only unjust aggressors and not whole peoples forfeit their rights and therefore become subject to despotical rule. This is because the people cannot transfer an unjust power to their government and therefore it is the government and its direct servants who must be held responsible for the breach of the moral law. There are of course problems involved in applying Locke's conception of just war to the total war of the twentieth century, yet at some level Locke's argument does apply in terms of different levels of responsibility. Yet even with those who forfeit their rights through aggression in an unjust war, it is only their right to life and liberty that is forfeit: the conqueror gains no right to their property or that of their descendants or family. This is because families retain a legitimate expectation to inherit and enjoy property – particularly property in land – and this cannot be forfeit even by the actions of an unjust aggressor. Of course it can be subject to charge, so the property of an unjust aggressor can be used to pay reparations for that aggression and for the costs of punishing that aggression in war. However, even here the conquerors' claim to just recompense cannot be so great as to force the family of an aggressor into death and destitution. In § 183 Locke considers the case of the relative claims of just reparation and the absolute needs of an aggressor's family and he concludes that the absolute need should prevail on the grounds of the Natural Law to preserve. The discussion of the rights of forfeiture and their connection to property is important for Locke as it undermines the claims of absolutists to base despotical rule on the basis of conquest. For Locke's crucial point is that despotical rule only extends over the persons of unjust aggressors and not their property; consequently it cannot give rise to jurisdiction over territory which would be central to any conception of sovereign political rule. To reinforce this point Locke considers whether a case for territorial jurisdiction could be based on just reparation for unjust aggression and his argument is no. Even if reparations were charged to the last farthing (the smallest unit of currency in Locke's day) this would at best give a few years' worth of the total national product of the society, but this would never extend to the value of the whole country in perpetuity. So reparations of the kind sought by the USSR against the defeated Germany in 1945 would still not justify the exercise of despotical jurisdiction over a country. Conquest cannot, therefore, provide a basis for legitimate political authority and cannot affect the terms of inheritance or land holding of the conquered population. In fact once a country has been conquered and unjust aggressors have been killed or punished and just reparations have been repaid the legitimate involvement of the conqueror ceases. One consequence of this is that the conqueror is not entitled to impose a new government on the conquered people. Only they can reconstitute a legitimate government for themselves and if the conqueror uses force to influence that outcome then it has no legitimacy at all as even agreements at the point of a sword or under duress have no force. The Hobbesian argument that conquest can be seen as a form of contract collapses and provides no challenge to the idea that legitimate government must always derive from the governed.

Usurpation

If the discussion of conquest involves (among many other things) an oblique warning against seeing the triumph of William and Mary as the opportunity for replacing a Catholic absolutism with a Protestant one, Locke's discussion of usurpation is also a similar warning. His concern is always to defend consent as the only source of legitimate political power, whoever might be exercising it. Therefore, although Locke is certainly more sympathetic to the cause of William of Orange than to James II, his personal political judgement has no relevance to deciding who exercises legitimate political authority. Conquest, even a good conquest resulting from a legitimate war, does not establish legitimate political rule.

Similarly in the case of usurpation, even if that happens to be a 'good' usurpation such as the replacement of the Catholic absolutism of James II with the Protestant rule of William of Orange, there is no legitimate transfer of power and therefore no right to rule.

Locke defines usurpation as a form of domestic conquest, where one party within the state takes control of the Executive and Legislative power of the state from another. In effect it involves a change of personnel in the Executive and Legislative. If this were to involve the replacement of the existing legitimate structure of the state then the usurpation would in effect be a war of aggression against the people and consequently it could not be a source of the right to rule. But even if the usurpation leaves the basic structure of the constitution as it is and merely involves a change of personnel, it still cannot be the basis of legitimate right and this would be so even if the new ruler were to respect the Natural Rights of his subjects. Locke's point is to remind us that the constitutional structure of the state is based on the consent of the people. We do not merely consent to enter political society and constitute ourselves as a people, we also agree in constituting ourselves as a people to be ruled in accordance with certain laws and institutions that specify who shall exercise political authority over us and on what terms. As we have seen Locke does not opt for a version of representative democracy, but he does argue that how the Executive and Legislative is chosen is part of the social contract that each succeeding generation is supposed to endorse through acts of express or tacit consent. Whatever those rules happen to be – whether the idea of primogeniture in a hereditary monarchy or by frequent elections from a certain social class, or by popular election from a universal suffrage – they are the rules chosen and endorsed by the people and can only be changed by popular consent. Any unilateral change to the terms of the social contract and the fundamental constitution of the state, whether this is benign or malign, threatens to liberate individuals from the idea of a law-governed polity and therefore threatens the whole idea of constitutionally limited government under law. Where such a change takes place, as we might argue happened during the Glorious Revolution of 1688, the legitimacy of the new Executive will still depend solely upon the consent of the governed and not on the act of usurpation itself. Given the way the discussion of conquest and usurpation entail both a warning about the new post-1688 settlement and a highly qualified endorsement of the new regime with the clear implication that its authority rests on the consent of the people, it is not surprising that Locke was so concerned to maintain anonymity of authorship of the *Second Treatise*.

Tyranny, rebellion and resistance

The discussion of conquest and usurpation provides an account of the illegitimate establishment of political regimes, but a more pressing question facing Locke is what we should do about illegitimate regimes when they exist. It is here that Locke is at his most radical and controversial as he argues we have a right to resist against illegitimate uses of political power and a right to rebel against regimes that threaten our rights and civil interests. This right is both an individual right and a collective right exercised on the part of the whole political community.

Locke begins his discussion of resistance and rebellion by defining the problem of tyranny. Tyranny is a popular term of disapproval of government and the term is often overused in political debates such that absolutists like Hobbes claim that it merely means any regime of which one disapproves. Locke wants to be more specific so defines tyranny as any 'exercise of power beyond right' (§ 199). As such any form of government can collapse into a tyranny and it is no longer, as it was for classical philosophers, merely a corruption of monarchy. He reinforces this point with the justly famous claim that remains at the heart of all liberal theories: '. . . wherever Law ends Tyranny begins . . .' (§ 202). The definition is simple and seems to need little further clarification as that has been provided by Locke's previous arguments in the *Second Treatise*. That said, we can identify at least four ways in which Locke suggests tyranny can be exercised and on the basis of which resistance and rebellion can be offered.

The first and most obvious case is when the prince or government fails to act within, and enforce, the Law of Nature. The most fundamental reason for joining together to form a political society and submitting oneself to political rule is the secure protection of one's Natural Rights. When any prince or his servant fails to act within these rights he is engaging in aggressive war against his subjects. In such circumstances the subject has both the right to resist and the right to punish a breach of the Law of Nature with action up to and including the infliction of the death penalty.

The second example is where the prince or government fails to act to protect the public good. The public good is not exhausted by the Natural Rights of the members of political society, but it is, as we have seen, constrained by those rights so that exercises of prerogative are justified in so far as they can be seen to support and defend those basic rights. Breaches of the public good would possibly include taxation without protection of the law or security of the state. Such forms of tyranny could therefore result as much from lack of care and competence as from ill will and malice towards the people.

The third example is in cases where the prince has lost the public trust (§ 221). As Lloyd-Thomas has argued, this condition entails a subjective condition of 'attitudinal consent' as the loss of trust has to be felt and believed by the populace and this might not occur even when there are serious breaches of the Law of Nature – as when a majority is indifferent to the oppression of a national minority.[26] Similarly, the breakdown of trust might occur even when there is no violation of the Natural Law or Rights. There is some debate among Locke scholars whether such a situation would entail a dissolution of government and grounds for legitimate resistance, yet at § 220 Locke is quite clear that the risk of falling into tyranny can provide an adequate ground for resistance. Presumably Locke's point is to do with the persistence of threats to breach the terms of political legitimacy. A case in point is the threat posed to the Protestant settlement by James II's open Catholicism and association with French absolutism. Locke's point is that the constant risk to the rights of Protestant Englishmen breaks down the necessary trust between governors and governed even before James II might have tried to convert England to Catholicism. Although Lloyd-Thomas is right to point out that the third form of tyranny is potentially in conflict with the others, Locke does suggest that the breach of trust has to be accompanied by breaches of a more threatening kind. The suggestion is that the breach of trust builds up as a result of small individual lawless actions which on their own are not grounds for the whole of society to consider government dissolved.

The fourth form of tyranny occurs when the rulers act outside of the positive law. This would include cases where a magistrate refuses to offer the equal protection of the laws by imposing similar punishments for similar crimes, or by acting corruptly to exempt certain parties from punishments prescribed by the law. We might also consider cases of usurpation under this form of tyrannical act, as that involves setting aside the constitutional procedures for replacing the Executive or Legislative and consequently breaches of the positive law.

The question that remains is what should one do about such exercises of 'power beyond right', and the subsequent discussion in the chapter on tyranny and the chapter on the dissolution of government (chapters XVIII and XIX) are devoted to that. Locke is taken to offer a defence of a right to rebel against an unjust exercise of power, and while this is undoubtedly the case his argument is complex. Just on the issue of whether the right is one of rebellion or resistance we can already see the complexity.

Locke does not think there is a right to rebel against a legitimately constituted state or a government acting with the law and its just discretion, despite the fact that the word 'rebellion' tends to be used in cases of illegitimate revolts against the state and its authority. This would seem to suggest that we only have a right to rebel against an unjust and illegitimate state or government. However, as Locke suggests through his choice of chapter title, a government that acts beyond the law effectively dissolves itself; therefore one can hardly rebel against it. This is reinforced by Locke's claim that the exercise of illegitimate force is an act of aggressive war (§ 207) and therefore that the people are perfectly within their rights to defend themselves and resist the aggression. Similarly he suggests that a prince or government that puts itself in a position of war with its people ceases to be the legitimate government, and are therefore the true rebels against the legitimate order. Again the people are within their rights to resist such rebels. All of this indicates that Locke is really concerned with a right of resistance and not of rebellion. However, this would not fully capture Locke's position for as we have seen the people can rebel when trust is irrevocably broken between people and government, a process that can be gradual and not follow any particular breach of rights or the law. Locke is careful not to confine the right to one of resisting only when the breach of right has taken place, as this would be no more than '. . . to bid them first be Slaves, and then to take care of their Liberty: and when their Chains are on, tell them, they may act like Freemen' (§ 220). The right is therefore not merely to '. . . get out of . . .' the unjust aggression, but also to prevent it and that might require the removal of an illegitimate or unjust government that poses a persistent threat to the liberties and rights of the people. It is precisely this idea that is captured in the idea of trust between government and people. Government has to exercise a necessary prerogative in deciding how it secures and protects the rights, liberties and civil interests of the people, and this cannot be done mechanically. Consequently some acts which are for the public good will seem to conflict with their protection and the promotion of the common good. As long as the governed trust the judgement of the government, these actions, policies or laws can fall within the legitimate discretion of the state without being a cause for dissolution. Yet the matter remains one of judgement. Levels of taxation will no doubt be controversial, especially if they are used to fund expensive foreign military adventures that have only an ever more remote connection with national security. Different individuals and groups will legitimately disagree about such policies without threatening the stability of government. That said, Locke also believed that there were other policies and actions which could not really be said to fall within the legitimate discretion of the Executive and Legislative power and which threatened a much greater assault of the rights of the governed. A good example which preoccupied Locke in a number of his writings was the imposition of a uniform religion against the conscience of the people. This is most clearly illustrated in Locke's *Letter Concerning Toleration* which was published at the same time as the *Second Treatise* and is his other great contribution to liberal political philosophy. The issue of religious conformity is a good example as this can be pursued by small increments, each one of which – such as kneeling, crossing oneself in church, or removing hats in religious services – might seem pretty innocuous and hardly worth taking up arms for. Yet taken together they potentially form part of a more substantial assault on religious liberty which is indeed a breach of the Law of Nature. In such cases taking up arms against the state would indeed be closer to rebellion, although it would also be resistance to a government that had dissolved itself through undermining the necessary trust between governed and rulers.

When to rebel and resist?

The final set of questions that Locke addresses in relation to the right of rebellion and resistance are the most complex and difficult. These concern when to rebel or resist and who decides. Locke discusses the issue from the perspective of the individual and from that of the society as a whole.

In the case of the individual Locke reasserts the individual's inalienable right to defend himself against forceful aggression, whether this is from a thief or murderer, or a government servant acting outside the law. The threat and use of force puts an aggressor in a state of war with the 'aggressee' and they retain the right to defend themselves and resist. In the case of robbers and thieves, Locke argues that the individual retains the right to punish breaches of the law as it would be unreasonable and unfeasible to rely on public authorities to come to your aid while being attacked at night. If the aggressor is the government or one of its functionaries then relying on the public defence is also impossible so one retains the right to resist. Yet in the case of individuals, Locke argues that the right to resist is only appropriate in the face of direct threats of force. If one can go to law to hold to account an unjust act by a public official, then one should do that first. If a magistrate fails to enforce a right, one should first seek appeal against that decision, and most jurisdictions allow for appeals and reviews of decisions up to the highest court. Locke does not want to turn every act that breaches the Law of Nature, positive law or the public good to become a reason for aggression because not all such acts will indicate the dissolution of government. Many such acts will be the result of officials acting *ultra vires* rather than the state collapsing into an unjust aggressor. Such cases will occur in legitimate states and therefore will not of themselves undermine the public trust. If however an individual falls foul of the state and cannot seek redress from its highest court or the king, this does not necessarily entail that the individual should go to war against the state. Individuals must use their reason and judge the likelihood of success of going to war against the state without the support of their fellows. Clearly if the state mounts an assault on a person's life and property then they have no choice but to defend themselves and probably nothing much to lose if they are unsuccessful. But in cases where a person's life may not be at risk or their person and property might not be at risk in perpetuity, one needs to exercise prudence. If such acts by the government become widespread or widely known they will potentially lead to the breach of public trust that generates a public reason to resist the government, but if the cases are few and not well known, the individual might find himself on his own and he must therefore exercise prudence. As Locke argues in § 208 it would be madness for one man to go to war against the state.

If assaults by government are more generally felt on the wider public, the situation is different and the case for regarding the government as dissolved is clearer. But even in this case Locke's argument is potentially problematic for we need some mechanism for deciding when the public trust has dissolved and when breaches of the law are so great as to become grounds for a just war against a rebel government. The simple answer to the problem of when a government has dissolved is provided by the idea of a majority judgement. As we have already seen, Locke relies on majority will to determine matters that fall within the remit of the Law of Nature, but which are not directly prescribed by appeal to our Natural Rights. In the case of the family we needed a principle of rule that is compatible with the rights of the two parties so Locke trusts to the stronger power and, in the case of deciding the form of constitution within a political society, he trusts to the stronger power, namely the numerical majority. Similarly in the case of deciding when the government has dissolved, we should appeal to the majority judgement. Yet this answer is far from straightforward in the case of the right to resist a rebel government.

The most obvious problem faced in relying on the judgement of the majority is how that is expressed. In establishing a political society the people create a constitutional procedure for choosing and replacing those who govern them, but in the case of a dissolved government this procedure is not available, and there does not seem to be an alternative structure available. This leaves the question of how we can distinguish a vocal and active minority from a genuine majority and how we can identify a majority when the margin between majority and minority is very small. Even in complex modern electoral systems it can be very difficult to distinguish the majority will or voice. How much more difficult is it to identify it in the face of a dissolution of government?

A further problem is what is to be done if the majority is actually indifferent to actions on the part of the government that ought to dissolve its legitimacy? Suppose the majority of a state allows its government to persecute, expropriate and kill its Jewish minority population. Each action is a clear breach of the Law of Nature, but if the majority sees these acts as solely confined to a minority it does not care about, it can easily claim that the general public trust is unaffected and therefore it will not judge the government to have been dissolved. Locke might well respond that as an objective matter the government is dissolved, but if the majority is sufficiently large and well armed there might be little or no prospect of success if the minority went to war against the majority. The point here is what is the help of appealing to the majority?

One might start to think that Locke's defence of a right of rebellion is starting to look rather empty as in the case of individuals it does little more than allow a right to self defence against direct violence and counsel caution against any other actions on the grounds of their likelihood of failure. And in the case of public rebellion Locke does not provide any easy mechanism for deciding when we can resist a rebel government. Yet before we dismiss his argument completely we need to note three things which perhaps rescue it from being vacuous.

First, we should recognize that although it is hard to identify the precise criteria for when a particular government has dissolved itself, and gone to war with its people, we can identify some cases in history and contemporary politics where the necessary and sufficient conditions of dissolution clearly obtain. In the case of Rwanda in 1994, where the majority Hutu population went to war against the minority Tutsi population, it would be hard to claim that the government continued to function as a legitimate government and had not dissolved itself into a warring faction. Such cases may be rare, but they do exist and they do combine clear breaches of the Law of Nature with a breakdown of public trust, however difficult it might have been to decide whether the Hutu aggressors represented the genuine majority will or not. We should not therefore dismiss Locke's argument as wholly unworkable.

Secondly, perhaps we should expect Locke's argument to give clear answers in only the most serious circumstances. Locke is quite clear that he does not want to license every disgruntled individual or group to go to war against the state. Indeed in §§ 224–8 Locke discusses the positive value of a doctrine of a right to rebellion in helping to secure social stability and order. The standard objection to arguments for a right to rebellion is that it will license all manner of 'busybodies' to upset the necessary order of the state and to ferment dispute. Hobbes makes this argument following the English Civil War which he thought was fermented by such people, and in the late eighteenth century Jeremy Bentham criticized the doctrine of the rights of man as 'terrorist language' for its tendency to dissolve the bonds of political obligation. These conservative arguments are supplemented by claims that the pains and chaos of dissolution are so great that it can never be worth overthrowing a government. As we have already seen, Locke is happy to challenge this complacency and to argue that sometimes security is worth sacrificing to achieve freedom and justice. But alongside the defence of liberty against security, Locke also advances the interesting claim that asserting a right to rebellion may well make the need to appeal to that right less and less necessary. Locke makes this point explicitly in § 226 where he says '. . . That *this Doctrine . . .* is *the best fence against Rebellion*, and the probablest means to hinder it'. Perhaps we should see the defence of the right to rebellion as a trump card that the people always hold against the government, and a potential warning about what might happen if they stray beyond lawful political power. If this checking function works properly, then it will rarely if ever need to be exercised. In this sense it is like the provision for emergency powers in a constitution, where the provision refers to the exercise of extra constitutional powers which by definition cannot be formalized in the normal structure of the law. In Locke's case the emergency power resides only with the people and not with a ruler. Interestingly Locke does not even include referral to a higher power such as God in his account of rebellion and resistance. Although breaches of the Law or Nature will ultimately be judged by God, Locke rejects the standard medieval argument that we must appeal to God when the monarch acts against the Law of Nature and the people. For Locke, the prince is not part of a divinely instituted order but is the creation of his people. Thus while individuals are always answerable for their actions, in judging the prince, appeal must be made to the people and not God (§ 204), again illustrating that while religious premises play an important role in Locke's argument we should not overstate their importance in determining every argument.

Locke's defence to the right of rebellion as the best protection against having to rebel against government poses a challenge back to conservatives such as Hobbes or Bentham. In the end the argument of both Locke and the conservatives turns on testable hypotheses, but ones where the evidence is never wholly conclusive. That said, if we do see Locke's argument as primarily addressed to government we should not be too surprised that it is difficult to cash out in practice and he is not primarily concerned with its practical use except in the most egregious cases of war against the people.

Yet there is one final consideration that we must note with respect to majority judgements about when government has dissolved. One of the problems alluded to above arises when a majority becomes indifferent to an assault of a minority. Yet can such a case occur in Locke's ideal theory? What I mean by this is whether we have a strict duty to defend each other against acts of aggression such that it is not a moral option for individuals to be indifferent to the sufferings of others within their political society.

That we have such a duty, and not merely a liberty to act or not as we wish, is clear from the terms of our constituting ourselves as a political society. The point of our doing so was to provide for the collective enforcement of our rights and the preservation of the common good. Part of this agreement is the acknowledgement of a duty to support and protect the rights of all other members of the political community in return for a similar protection from others. In these circumstances we have a duty to protect other members of our society who are being assaulted by the rebel government where this duty is not a matter of discretion or liberty. This duty is especially important, as Locke is keen to emphasize that it is the government and not the political society that is dissolved by such *ultra vires* actions – we do not get thrown back into a State of Nature where we have no collective responsibility for our neighbours. In this sense we do indeed have a duty to support those who are being attacked by the state and for this reason it might be much easier to infer a majority judgement against the government if their abuses are particularly gross. But what also follows from this is that we have no right to be indifferent to the sufferings of a minority within our own state if we face up to our obligations properly and furthermore if there are indeed social facts about us which make us tend to form political societies with certain people and not others, we are unlikely to find ourselves in legitimate political societies with those whom we are wholly indifferent about.

Locke of course does not have a theory of the social bases of modern states, neither does he have a conception of the nation or a people that subsequent political theorists have used to explain why there are particular historical states and to explain the basis of social cooperation within states. This is no doubt a potential failing that subsequent theories have made much of at the expense of Locke's voluntarist individualism. Yet where much subsequent political theory tended to reject the normative rationalism of Locke's theory in favour of explanatory theories of political and civil society, Locke's normative account of legitimacy remains important as we find states claiming the right to oppress and even exterminate parts of their population. It is certainly the case that an adequate theory of the state needs to balance the claims of individual rights and the social basis of cooperation and sociability. Yet in the last resort Locke's defence of individuals' unique moral importance and the duty of political societies to protect that importance whatever the persons' beliefs, culture or values, remains a powerful lesson, whatever the weaknesses or inadequacies of his particular arguments. And it is for this reason that Locke remains a major inspiration for many subsequent liberal political philosophers, even when they reject or abandon many of those arguments.

CHAPTER 4

RECEPTION AND INFLUENCE

i LOCKE'S INFLUENCE IN THE EIGHTEENTH AND NINETEENTH CENTURIES

For much of the life of the book the *First* and *Second Treatises* were detached, with the *Second Treatise* being the most widely read. Indeed as early as 1691 an edition, prepared by David Mazel, a Huguenot pastor in exile in Holland, appeared which had dropped the *First Treatise* and the Preface and which re-ordered the remaining work in numbered chapters rather than continuously numbered paragraphs. This version became one of the most influential versions of Locke's text and it is largely in this version that the text comes down through successive centuries and through which Locke's status as a classic thinker of modern political philosophy emerged. It is also through this edition that Locke appears as a founder of the liberal constitutionalism that is enshrined in the American Founders' Constitution. And it is through the terms of this interpretation of Locke as the inspiration of American-style liberal constitutionalism, an interpretation that gathered momentum in the nineteenth century, that many still see him today. Yet much recent Locke scholarship has been devoted to overturning this liberal view of Locke as the father of constitutional democracy (and more importantly as an inspiration for the American Revolution) and rehabilitating the *First Treatise* as an essential part of his political theory in the *Two Treatises of Civil Government*. Before turning to a brief outline of contemporary interpretations of Locke's *Second Treatise*, I want to examine the fortunes of Locke's book in the immediate aftermath of its publication.

Locke's immediate legacy is somewhat complicated. Until recently many scholars regarded the *Second Treatise* as a statement and defence of the Revolution principles of 1688. These principles were then handed down through the eighteenth century to the American Revolutionaries and by way of Tom Paine (1737–1809) to France of 1791 and the English radicalism of the early nineteenth century. Yet this picture is too simple. First, as we have seen, Locke composed the *Second Treatise* in the early 1680s; that is before the English Revolution had happened. It could be neither a prediction of the outcome of a set of events that from early 1680s would have seemed pretty unlikely, nor a manifesto for those events. Secondly, Locke chose to publish the work anonymously and was strict in ensuring it remained anonymous until after his death in 1704. If his work was a vindication of the Glorious Revolution this strategy would not have been necessary and would indeed have been strange. The likely explanation for Locke's reticence in claiming authorship is that the *Two Treatises*, and the *Second Treatise* in particular, advanced a far more radical position than that embodied in the Revolution settlement. For many the Revolution was nothing of the sort but was merely the acceptance of a vacant throne by William of Orange who was related to the royal line by marriage. Locke's more radical argument claims that political authority ultimately derives from the consent of the governed and more controversially that the governed have a right to rebel when the monarch breaches the trust given him by the government. This is precisely the sort of dangerous doctrine the new regime would have feared.

Following Locke's death the authorship of the work became known and it was an object of criticism from parties who wished to challenge the more radical doctrines of the Whig party in Parliament.

Locke's radical reputation caused the *Second Treatise* to be singled out as a dangerous document, but Locke's reputation as a whole depended on more than that work. His *Essay Concerning Human Understanding*, published at the same time, was the main vehicle through which his reputation spread. While this book established his reputation as a central figure of the philosophy of Enlightenment that had developed by the mid-eighteenth century, at the same time his abstract, rationalistic and radical political ideas were displaced by other currents of thought that drew on history, law and civic republican ideas during the same period.[1]

The impact of his *Second Treatise* in the remainder of the eighteenth century is difficult to trace with precision, as different aspects of his arguments fared better than others. Undoubtedly the idea of government based on consent and the idea of natural rights played some part in the intellectual ferment of the American founding. But Locke's ideas were only one source, and a source that was carefully disaggregated. Locke's defence of private property and its rights was pretty much common currency in many political theories which would have rejected other aspects of his thought, so it is difficult to point to a strong principled defence of property rights as evidence of Locke's influence. Similarly Locke's ideas on the separateness of powers are also part of the common currency of the American Founding, but these ideas are also found throughout the classical republican tradition and in French writers such as Montesquieu, who rejected the abstractness of Lockean rights theory.

One idea central to Locke's argument in the *Second Treatise* did not play a significant role in the debates surrounding the American Revolution or in similar debates in Europe in the late eighteenth century and that is the idea that political societies are ultimately based on an original social contract. By the mid-eighteenth century the use of an original contract had come under significant attack, first by the Scottish philosopher David Hume (1711–76) and J-J. Rousseau (1712–78). Rousseau's *Discourse on the Origin of Inequality* (1755) attacked the State of Nature arguments on which social contract theories such as Locke's depended. For Rousseau the State of Nature merely reflected the vices of contemporary society in a false account of the natural condition. Hume's argument was addressed towards the contract basis of political society and the use of consent arguments to justify political obligation. Hume's argument developed in the *Treatise of Human Nature* and a short essay 'Of the Original Contract' was so devastating that the use of the social contract fell out of use in English-speaking political philosophy until it was resurrected by John Rawls in the 1970s.[2]

Hume's argument was that the social contract was not only historically naive, as no one could ever find evidence of such a contract, but also that it was incoherent to base the idea of obligation on a contract, as the whole idea of a contract was a complex social convention that already depended on the idea of obligation. It made no sense to appeal to contract to explain obligations, such as our obligation to obey the law or the state, as these already depended on social practices that must have legitimacy independently of a contract. The question then arose how and why such practices came about and in order to answer this Hume made an appeal to the idea of utility. This idea is present but not fully theorized in Locke's conception of tacit consent, whereby it is argued that the enjoyment of the benefits of a society is itself grounds of political obligation as a form of consent. Hume's argument follows Locke's but without the redundant appeal to the concept of consent. Although not himself a utilitarian in any straightforward sense, Hume's appeal to the doctrine of utility and its subsequent development at the hands of Jeremy Bentham (1748–1832) and John Stuart Mill (1806–73) marginalized Locke's rights-based contractarianism within subsequent political philosophy. The dominance of utilitarianism and the negative effect of the republican terror of the French Revolution on the doctrine of the Rights of Man had done much to limit Locke's influence – he is rarely mentioned in the work of Bentham or J. S. Mill.

Yet while Locke's *Second Treatise* went into a period of philosophical neglect in the nineteenth century, during the same period there was a renewed interest in Locke as a source of the Whig settlement of 1688. It is precisely during this nineteenth-century period that the idea of Locke as the apologist for the Glorious Revolution and as the ideologist of the subsequent American Revolution gained ground in the works of historians such as Macaulay, H. R. Fox-Bourne and Sir Leslie Stephen. Thomas Babington Macaulay was particularly keen to defend a Whig political theory that defended a liberal and accountable government but which rejected the radical appeals for extending the suffrage that were emerging from the philosophic radicals associated with Bentham. This task was no doubt in part inspired by the need to rescue Locke from the hands of radicals such as Paine and Richard Price (1723–91) and co-opt him into a mainstream tradition of English liberty that connected the Glorious Revolution of 1688 with the triumph of the British political and imperial power in the mid-nineteenth century. The fact that this model of power had little to do with deriving political authority from the governed, especially given the expansion of British imperial power in India following the loss of the North American colonies, seems not to have troubled Macaulay and his Whig followers.

As we shall see in the next section, it was precisely this Whig view of history and Locke's place in it that inspired much of the historical work on Locke and his context in the mid-twentieth century. One happy consequence of the nineteenth-century reading of Locke was that it inspired a return to Locke scholarship leading to Fox-Bourne's two-volume biography of Locke and the recovery and publication of important Locke manuscripts.

There is one final and somewhat curious acknowledgement of Locke's argument during the nineteenth century that deserves mention, as it will have a bearing on some of the debates surrounding Locke's work in the twentieth century, and that is in the work of Karl Marx. In *The German Ideology*, Marx provides a critique of the alienation and exploitation of the capitalist system. In particular he focuses on the wage-labour system as alienating the labourer from the product of his labour, which in turn transforms labour as the defining feature of man's species being into a form of tyranny and oppression. Underlying all of this is the labour theory of value, or the idea that it is man's transformation of brute nature that gives it value and significance. This as we have seen is a central component of Locke's theory of initial property acquisition in Chapter V of the *Second Treatise*. Marx accepts that labour is the source of value as this is necessary for his account of exploitation as the driving spirit of capitalism. However, he rejects Locke's use of the wage-labour system following the introduction of money as a basis for an equal right to acquire property, as he claims the property of the wage-labourer is the source of the labourer's own oppression.[3]

Marx may well get much of Locke's argument wrong, but he does appreciate the complex interrelationship between freedom, property, labour and contract that was central to Locke's conception of civil society. Furthermore, Marx does not fully appreciate the extent to which nineteenth-century economic theory moved away from labour theories of value to welfare or utility-based theories under the influence of J. S. Mill. All that said, it remains interesting that one of the continuing inspirations to read Locke's political theory in the *Second Treatise* comes from a thinker who rejects the whole notion of private property on which Locke built his conception of civil society and government. This fascination with Locke from the political left has continued into the twentieth century through the likes of C. B. Macpherson and more recently G. A. Cohen, and in the writings of early twentieth-century historians of political thought such as Harold Laski, the Marxist critique of private property and the wage-labour system is combined with the Whig interpretation of history found in Macauley.

By the end of the nineteenth century Locke's rights theory and contractarianism had consigned his political philosophy to an historical curiosity as opposed to a widely shared public philosophy, such as Bentham and Mill's utilitarianism. Yet the nineteenth-century turn from the abstractions of Natural Rights theory towards a more historically based conception of political theory had also inspired a continued interest in Locke's place in political thought amongst both liberals and radicals such as Marx. This preoccupation with the historical place of Locke in the development of Western political theory was to become one of the major preoccupations of Locke scholars in the twentieth century.

ii HISTORY, RELIGION AND LOCKE – CONTEMPORARY INTERPRETATIONS OF LOCKE

The publication in 1960 of Peter Laslett's magisterial scholarly edition of the *Two Treatises*, and the subsequent historical interpretations of Locke's argument by John Dunn, Richard Ashcraft and John Marshall, among many others, have challenged the idea that Locke was the father of the American Revolution or that he provided the theoretical blueprint for the American Founding. The challenge to such a-historical readings of the *Second Treatise* has partly consisted of alternative interpretations of Locke's impact in the decades following his death in 1704, some of which we have reviewed in the previous section. But the new historical interpretations have also drawn on debates about the methodology, or the appropriate way to read the writings of great political theorists, inspired by movements in twentieth-century political philosophy and criticisms of rival, reductionist theories such as those offered by Marxist scholars.

Philosophers have always benefited from the work of historians who provide them with authoritative texts from which they can then work. Yet the recovery of the *First Treatise* as part of the *Two Treatises of Government*, and the debates surrounding the relationship and composition of the two works, have contributed to a resurgence of interest in the relationship between history and philosophy, and advanced a strong argument for the primacy of historical over philosophical understandings of arguments, if not actually denying the possibility of distinctly philosophical interpretations of the arguments of thinkers from the past. The implication of Laslett's scholarship and that of many who have followed him, albeit disagreeing with details of his argument, is that if we try and distil the purely philosophical theory from Locke's *Two Treatises*, from the contingencies of biography and context of the sort discussed in Chapter 1, then we actually distort Locke's arguments and misunderstand his theory. In other words we cannot simply set out the life of an author and then turn to a separate and distinct realm in which his ideas exist, one that is untouched by his life and context. We have to see the ideas and the context as inextricably related. Only in this way, according to Laslett, will we avoid a number of crass errors, such as seeing Locke as a modern constitutional liberal and his argument as a response to the absolutist contractarianism of Thomas Hobbes' *Leviathan* (1651).

As this modern contextualist tendency of collapsing philosophy into history has been rejected as the methodology of this book, we should devote some attention to understanding its central theses and because it will help understand how the approach offered in this book distinguishes it from that adopted by much recent Locke scholarship.

Those who wish to bring philosophy and history together into a historical discipline are often called contextualists, and we shall look at alternative contextualist approaches below. But before doing so we need to clarify what is meant by contextualism. There are two basic senses in which we can refer to context. The first is the social and economic context and the second is the intellectual context. The former kind of contextualism is closely associated with Marxist theories of ideology, and in Locke studies with the work of C. B. Macpherson.[4] For Macpherson, Locke's argument is a version of 'possessive individualism'; as such it both reflects the social form of the emerging capitalist mode of production and provides an indirect justification of the relations of production that go with emerging capitalism. To support this interpretation, he argues, we can appeal to the historical conditions in which Locke wrote with the growth of commercial society, colonial expansion abroad and enclosures in agriculture at home, as well as Locke's own interest in trade and stock-holding. The Marxist's point is a causal one, in that it claims that all ideas are ultimately a reflection of the relations of production and these are determined by the level and organization of the productive forces of a society. The key point here is that the context is external to the ideas themselves, as it refers to the social and economic forces that cause discourse and forms of debate to arise at different historical points. The problem with such external contextualist approaches is that they both overdetermine and underdetermine philosophical theories and texts. They overdetermine them by reducing theories to a crude reflection of class interest in the relations of production of capitalist society, so that Locke can be no more than an apologist for the new capitalist class. This is a simplification of the Marxist view of ideology which sees all thought as 'epiphenomenal'; that is, secondary to the causal forces that shape social relations. As all thought is ultimately a reflection of social relations that are determined or caused by the productive relations of that society, they will either be supportive of the existing order or critical of the existing order – in this case either endorsing the rise of the capitalist bourgeoisie or opposing it. Macpherson's argument is merely a more sophisticated version of the kind of history of liberalism that was offered by the likes of Harold Laski in the mid-twentieth century and which is still to be found in the work of socialist critics of liberalism such as Anthony Arblaster.

However, this approach also underdetermines such texts and theories because it fails to explain precisely why the arguments take the form they do. In other words it confuses the question of what an author is intending to do in taking up his pen and what he is intending (meaning) in saying something the way he does. One might be intending to earn money, curry favour or gain a job in deciding to write a book, but that is a very different thing from the question of what an author is intending by claiming that all political authority is based on consent. Knowing that an author needs a job or a meal will leave us uninformed about why he might distinguish between express and tacit forms of consent; consequently arguments such as Macpherson's appear to answer the wrong questions and leave the intellectual questions about the structure and meaning of Locke's arguments unaddressed. For interpreters such as Laski, Macpherson, and to some extent Arblaster, the question posed by Locke's theory is which side is he on, in the great struggle between Labour and Capital. Richard Ashcraft offers a more complex historical methodology than Macpherson, albeit one that still resembles the Marxist view of political theory as ideology, but interestingly he concludes that Locke might well have been far more sympathetic to the interests of Labour, so that even if we accept the terms of the Marxist debate it is not obvious that we must see Locke as an apologist for capitalism.

The arguments of Laski and Macpherson assume that the only interesting question to be asked in interpreting Locke's theory is which side he is on in respect of this issue. It begs the question by assuming that both alternative positions are reflections of conflicting class interests, and ignores the fact that the Locke's opponents might not simply be the interest of Labour or Capital but opponents in a completely different set of debates. Of course sophisticated Marxists might concede this last point and claim that all debates, even those concerning theological matters or issues in the emergence of the natural sciences, are determined by the mode of production of society. That may well be true, although it would be difficult to falsify and therefore could not be a knowledge claim, but even then it fails to offer any real explanation of what Locke was doing and why.

It is for this reason that such causal approaches have been replaced by or supplemented with alternative approaches that focus on the linguistic or intellectual context of texts and theories. These forms of contextualism draw our attention away from causal questions about why x did y and instead focuses our attention on the alternative question of what x intended by y or what an author meant by saying what he said. This form of contextualism is hermeneutic in that it is concerned with interpreting the meaning of a text (that is what hermeneutics means) and it grows out of the common experience that philosophical texts and arguments like any other form of literature are not immediately transparent. If texts were self-interpreting and transparent to readers, books such as this would be redundant, as they would merely repeat what Locke had already said.

If we take the social and economic contextualism of Marxists such as Macpherson as our first form of contextualism, we can also distinguish an alternative version, associated with the work of the Locke scholar John Dunn. Dunn rejects the causal reductionism of arguments such as Macpherson's.

Dunn's concern is with what he calls the identity of an argument.[5] Basically this is the question of what makes an interpretation an accurate account of what Locke actually thought and not merely what a later thinker imposes on Locke's argument. The question of identity here is what makes something what it is and not something else. When studying Locke's thought, Dunn argues that we have a moral obligation to attend to what Locke actually thought and not merely our own ideas of what he would have thought had he been a late twentieth-century constitutional liberal writing in Britain or the United States or a partisan on a Marxist debate between the interests of Labour and Capital. In part this obligation arises because Locke went to a lot of trouble trying to make his own distinctive arguments, and partly because the process of understanding itself involves attentiveness to what others are trying to say. In ordinary conversation understanding the other participant is an underlying moral imperative. Someone who never listens, always tries to complete someone else's sentences, or puts words into the mouth of another, is thought of as rude. The same idea in a more sophisticated guise underlies the task of historical interpretation and understanding. We do not have to read Locke, and we can do our own political thinking for ourselves, so in so far as we do engage with his texts we should try and be attentive to what he is doing. This entails that our primary approach to a philosophical text should be historical. Before we can connect Locke's argument to some perennial or timeless question such as the nature of political obligation or some social question about the distribution of economic power, we need to examine whether this is what Locke is actually concerned with. Similarly before we can criticize the logic of Locke's argument we need to know whether it is indeed Locke's argument and not merely some intellectual 'straw man' constructed as a heuristic device. The primacy of the historical over the philosophical interpretation of arguments means that we need to be attentive to the intellectual context in which Locke wrote in order to identify his argument. This context is the intricate web of ideas against which Locke is responding and in terms of which he is making his own particular arguments. It is clear from the previous chapters that the target of Locke's arguments was the refutation of the patriarchal theory of Sir Robert Filmer as opposed to the contractarian absolutism of Thomas Hobbes, as Filmer is the subject of the *First Treatise*. Dunn also chooses to emphasize the role of religion in the development of Locke's arguments and the extent to which he is a recognizably Christian thinker. Dunn's most important book on Locke, *The Political Thought of John Locke*, is an illustration of the 'linguistic contextualism' that he was one of the first to champion, but it also makes a substantive contribution to the interpretation of Locke's thought by emphasizing the indispensability of religion in Locke's argument. Dunn's concern is to challenge the view of Locke as a proto-liberal thinker by showing how intricately Locke's arguments about politics are connected with his primary theological concerns. The point is not merely to show how Locke's account of natural law is based on a theological premise, but rather he is concerned to show that the problem that motivated Locke's foray into political theory was derived from religious debates concerning comprehension and toleration, as well as Charles and James Stuart's Catholicism. Unless we understand that context we cannot understand why Locke is concerned to defend a right to rebellion. Followers of Dunn have continued to emphasize the importance of religion and religious debates to the character of Locke's mind. Ian Harris, for example, claims that unless we take the matter of Locke's theological commitments seriously we fail to understand a deeply religious thinker whose last works were on the *Reasonableness of Christianity* and the interpretation of the epistles of St Paul. It is not simply that Locke wrote in a religious age, he was a deeply religious man.

All of this is again designed to warn us against seeing Locke as either a closet sceptic ushering in an anti-religious Enlightenment culture, as some commentators influenced by Leo Strauss continue to claim, or as a proto-liberal whose ideas about rights, property and the limits of politics provide a blueprint for a liberal constitutional order such as that of the United States of America.

It is interesting to note that the arguments of scholars such as Dunn and Harris suggest that Locke's religious beliefs and commitments make him a peculiarly alien voice in modern politics and therefore a thinker who can teach us nothing about how to address our own political problems – a view I have sought to challenge throughout this book. These thinkers suggest, as do the followers of Leo Strauss, that we live in a deeply secular age that cannot make a place for religion in its public philosophy. The difference is that Strauss lays part of the blame for this secular culture on the writings of Locke. Yet this idea that the contemporary public philosophy of liberal and democratic societies must be secular has been challenged, not least by a number of Locke scholars.

Jeremy Waldron has recently suggested that Locke's religious defence of the role of fundamental equality can tell contemporary liberals a lot about the inadequacies of their own philosophical positions. Contemporary liberal political philosophers such as John Rawls and Ronald Dworkin have attempted to construct neutralist theories of political society, that is theories which remain neutral about questions concerning the fundamental truths of religion.

These theories do not set out to make the sceptical claim that traditional religion (such as Christianity) is false, but the more subtle claim that a public philosophy for a modern democratic society must avoid an appeal to religious beliefs and values in its fundamental arguments. Waldron's claim is that this neutralist strategy leaves liberals with nothing to say about their most basic premise – namely the fundamental freedom and equality of each person. Waldron does not go on to argue that modern liberal theories need to be supplemented by a traditional Protestant version of Christianity, although that has been how some of Waldron's critics have interpreted his argument. Instead he appeals to the role played by theological premises in Locke's argument to explain precisely what is missing from contemporary liberal theories and the form that the basic egalitarian premise must take.[6]

More recently, Greg Forster has gone further than Waldron and argued that Locke's particular version of Protestant Christianity is a good model for accommodating the pluralism and differences of modern democratic societies. Where Dunn and his followers claimed that Locke's religious beliefs made him irrelevant to modern debates about basic rights, social justice and the accommodation of diversity, Forster makes the opposite claim that it is precisely Locke's religious commitments that make him relevant, particularly in political societies such as that of the USA where there is a widespread acceptance of the form of Protestantism advocated by Locke. It is very difficult to decide on the basis of a reading of Locke's texts who is right and who is wrong. After all the question turns not only on the interpretation of Locke's texts but the claim that his society is fundamentally different from our own. If one sees modern society as a primarily secular society then there is undoubtedly a difference. However, secularism is a matter of degree and one of the claims that Forster makes is that the contrast between Locke's world and our own is often overblown. This is not a simple historical claim and therefore cannot be settled by showing how important religious premises are to Locke and how they do not appear in the work of contemporary liberals such as Rawls or Dworkin.[7]

iii LOCKE, PROPERTY AND CONTEMPORARY LIBERALISM

The preoccupation among many recent scholars with Locke's religious beliefs and commitments has been partly inspired by a desire to challenge the Marxist view of Macpherson that Locke was merely concerned with supporting the emergent capitalists of the late seventeenth century, and with showing that Locke could have very little to contribute to contemporary liberal societies. The liberal society that Locke was supposed to support was the constitutional settlement of the American Founding. This interpretation has fallen from favour, though it is still found in some recent commentators. However, as one version of Lockean liberalism has fallen from favour among scholars, Locke's arguments in the *Second Treatise* have been co-opted into another liberal tradition.

In 1974 the American philosopher Robert Nozick published *Anarchy, State and Utopia*, a work that has inspired a resurgence of interest in Locke and the foundations of property rights. Nozick opens his book with the striking claim that 'Individuals have rights, and there are things no person or group may do to them (without violating their rights). So strong and far reaching are these rights that they raise the question of what, if anything, the state and its officials may do.'[8] The claim that individuals have rights and that these are pre-political and place limits on the nature and extent of government self-consciously reflects a Lockean view of the basis of political legitimacy. Nozick's argument is developed in response to John Rawls' *A Theory of Justice*, published in 1971. Rawls initiated a return to normative political theory; that is, theory concerned with what the state ought to be and ought to do, following a long period of almost a century in which utilitarianism had dominated liberal democratic political discourse. Utilitarianism, as we have seen, developed in the eighteenth century in the decades following Locke's *Second Treatise* and by the nineteenth century it had come to eclipse a rights-based view of political thought. By the late nineteenth and early twentieth century utilitarianism had transformed most normative questions about the legitimacy and extent of political rule into technical questions about the levels of welfare provided by different policy options. Thus questions about whether the state should interfere with freedom of contract and impose a welfare state or whether it should leave welfare provision to a free market all collapsed into technical questions about which policy delivers most utility of welfare. Rawls challenged the primacy of utilitarianism by claiming that it failed to take seriously the separateness of persons. By this he meant that utilitarianism could countenance the violation of the rights of some for the good of a majority. A person-respecting theory would preclude such trade-offs. This idea, according to Rawls, is central to the tradition of liberal democratic thought and the idea of the primacy of rights that we find in the US Bill of Rights or the contemporary UN Declaration on Human Rights. As an alternative to utilitarianism Rawls offers an account of political and social legitimacy in terms of an egalitarian theory of social justice which distributes the conditions of freedom and fair equality of opportunity to each member of society.

While Nozick accepts Rawls' critique of utilitarianism on the grounds that it fails to take seriously the separateness or primacy of the person, he rejects in equal measure Rawls' alternative theory of social justice. Where Rawls derives his concept of civil and political rights from the primacy of his two principles of justice, Nozick, as we have seen, makes the rights claims fundamental. But he does more than this: he also argues that an appeal to person-respecting rights must preclude the kind of redistribution required by Rawls' theory, as this would violate the property rights that individuals have prior to political society. This does not mean that Nozick rejects the idea of justice, but it does mean that he has a conception of justice based on prior entitlement which rules out any coercive transfers of property within a state. Nozick famously argues that taxation is no better than 'forced labour'. If we have the kind of rights that Nozick claims are essential to explain the separateness of the person then there is no further room for social justice or taxation without consent. This argument echoes Locke's concern that Filmerian absolutism would allow the king to tax without consent and take property as he needed. But Nozick's argument does not merely echo Lockean themes. Nozick goes on to explore aspects of Locke's argument for the nature of political authority and most famously Locke's account of initial acquisition as the basis of a pre-political right to property.

Nozick's arguments are complex and controversial and are addressed as much to issues raised by Rawls and utilitarianism as they are by Locke's ideas – arguably the fundamental basis of Nozick's argument is provided by the eighteenth-century German philosopher Immanual Kant as much as by Locke – that said, they have had a significant impact on Locke scholarship and wider political debate. Many of Nozick's arguments have introduced Locke's ideas to a new-right political movement that was particularly influential in the 1980s in the US with Ronald Reagan and in the UK and Europe with Margaret Thatcher. The idea of a limited state, concerned to protect rights to freedom and private property, formed an important reaction to the ideas of a welfare state pursuing social redistribution ahead of individual rights. This Lockean view has continued to appeal to many in the recently 'liberated' countries of Eastern Europe where social justice is associated with Soviet-style command economies.

Nozick's depiction of Locke as a libertarian philosopher of the minimal state and strong defender of private property obviously appeals to a strand in American political culture, but it has challenged many to go back to Locke and see how far his defence of pre-political property rights supports Nozickean libertarianism. The desire to re-contextualize Locke's writings and weaken their support for Nozick's libertarian politics has led some commentators such as James Tully to interpret Locke's theory of property rights in a highly communitarian form, whereby individuals are required to support the worst off as a condition of owning anything. Tully's interpretation, though challenging, has not attracted much scholarly support. Other scholars such as Waldron and Ryan have nevertheless done much to explore the intricacies of Locke's argument, no doubt partly inspired by the felt need to challenge Nozick and defend Locke. Other political philosophers have tried to show that a careful reconstruction of Locke's argument can lead to un-Lockean conclusions. The Marxist philosopher G. A. Cohen has challenged at length the idea of self-ownership that is claimed to be at the heart of Locke's and Nozick's arguments. More recently, self-consciously left-libertarians such as Michael Otsuka have attempted to connect aspects of Locke's libertarianism with egalitarianism. While many continue to claim that this is either a dead-end for contemporary liberal political theory, or a distraction from the historical task of explaining what Locke meant in his complex writings, these debates do illustrate the extent to which Locke's arguments in the *Second Treatise* continue to shape our political self-understanding. It might well remain the case, as John Dunn claims, that we can learn few answers to contemporary problems by consulting Locke's work. We can, however, learn much about ourselves from reading the *Second Treatise* and if for no other reason that will continue to ensure that Locke's *Second Treatise* remains a work of political philosophy of the first rank.

NOTES

CHAPTER 1: LOCKE'S *SECOND TREATISE* IN CONTEXT

1. For a recent account of contemporary liberal theory see Kelly, P. (2004), *Liberalism*, Cambridge: Polity Press.
2. The 'Essay on Toleration' remained in manuscript and was ultimately overtaken by Locke's later published *Letters on Toleration*. A version of the *Essay* appeared in 1876 and a definitive scholarly edition was not published until 2006. See Locke, J. (2006), *Essay on Toleration*, J. Milton and P. Milton (eds), Oxford: Clarendon Press.
3. The two most important 'contextualist' historians of political thought for our purposes are John Dunn and Quentin Skinner. See Dunn, J. (1980), 'The Identity of the History of Ideas', in J. Dunn, *Political Obligation in its Historical Context*, Cambridge: Cambridge University Press, pp. 13–28; Skinner develops his argument in a variety of articles and books but the most important and widely discussed statement remains Skinner, Q. (1969), 'Meaning and Understanding in the History of Ideas', *History and Theory*, 8, 199–215.
4. Dunn, for example, argues that Christianity plays such a role in Locke's political theory that it can have almost nothing to teach late twentieth-century democratic societies, see Dunn, J. (1969), *The Political Thought of John Locke*. Dunn's view is challenged to some extent by Jeremy Waldron who concedes the importance of Christian arguments in Locke's work, especially concerning his premise of basic equality between moral subjects, but who goes on to argue that we can still learn much from Locke, see Waldron, J. (2002), *God, Locke and Equality: Christian Foundations in Locke's Political Thought*, Cambridge: Cambridge University Press.

CHAPTER 2: OVERVIEW AND KEY THEMES

1. Laslett, P. (1988), Introduction, in J. Locke, *Two Treatises of Government*, Cambridge: Cambridge University Press.

2. Strauss, L. (1953), *Natural Right and History*, Chicago: University of Chicago Press.
3. See Waldron (2002), *God, Locke and Equality*.

CHAPTER 3: READING THE TEXT

1. Locke was primarily concerned with the claims of Charles II and James II, yet belief in the divine right of kingship was shared with Charles and James' father Charles I and their grandfather James I (and IV of Scotland). James I, being of a more reflective cast of mind than his son or grandsons, was the author of one of the most important defences of the divine right of kings, *The True Law of Free Monarchies* (1603).
2. See Filmer, Sir. Robert (1991), *Patriarcha' and Other Writings*, Sommerville, J. P. (ed.), Cambridge: Cambridge University Press.
3. Nozick, Robert (1974), *Anarchy, State and Utopia*, Oxford: Basil Blackwell, p. ix.
4. Hobbes, Thomas, *Leviathan* [1651], Chapter XIII.
5. Singer, Peter (1977), *Animal Liberation*, London: Jonathan Cape.
6. Waldron, Jeremy (2002), *God, Locke and Equality*, ch. 3.
7. Berlin, Isaiah (1969), 'Two Concepts of Liberty', in *Four Essays on Liberty*, Oxford: Oxford University Press.
8. Forster, Greg (2005), *John Locke's Politics of Moral Consensus*, Cambridge: Cambridge University Press.
9. Hohfeld, W. N. (1919), *Fundamental Legal Conceptions As Applied to Judicial Reasoning*, New Haven: Yale University Press.
10. Simmons, A. John (1992), *A Lockean Theory of Rights*, Princeton: Princeton University Press, ch. 2.
11. Dunn, John (1969), *The Political Thought of John Locke*; Ashcraft, Richard (1987), *Locke's Two Treatises of Government*, London: Unwin Hyman; and Tully, James (1980), *A Discourse on Property*, Cambridge: Cambridge University Press.
12. Strauss, L. (1953), *Natural Right and History*, Chicago: University of Chicago Press; Cox, Richard (1960), *Locke on War and Peace*, Oxford: Clarendon Press.
13. Nozick, Robert (1974), *Anarchy, State and Utopia*, pp. 290–2.
14. Lloyd-Thomas, David (1995), *Locke on Government*, London: Routledge, p. 89.
15. Cohen, G. A. (1995), *Self-Ownership, Freedom and Equality*, Cambridge: Cambridge University Press; Otsuka, Michael (2003), *Libertarianism without Inequality*, Oxford: Oxford University Press.
16. Day, J. P. (1966), 'Locke on Property', *Philosophical Quarterly*, vol. 16, pp. 207–20; Waldron, Jeremy (1988), *A Right to Private Property*, Oxford: Clarendon Press, pp. 184–91.
17. Nozick, Robert (1974), *Anarchy, State and Utopia*, p. 175.
18. Laski, Harold. J. (1996), *The Rise of European Liberalism*, New Brunswick NJ: Transaction Publishers; Macpherson, C. B. (1962), *The*

Political Theory of Possessive Individualism, Oxford: Oxford University Press.

19. Cohen, G. A. (1995), *Self-Ownership, Freedom and Equality*, ch. 10.
20. Pateman, Carole (1988), *The Sexual Contract*, Cambridge: Polity Press.
21. See Locke, J. (1689), *Letter Concerning Toleration*, in J. Horton and S. Mendus (eds). (1991), *John Locke – A Letter Concerning Toleration in Focus*, London: Routledge, p. 46.
22. Nozick, Robert (1974), *Anarchy, State and Utopia*, pp. 10–25.
23. Mill, J. S. (1991), *On Liberty*, in J. Gray (ed.), *John Stuart Mill On Liberty and Other Essays*, Oxford: World Classics, p. 8.
24. Horton, J. (1992), *Political Obligation*, Basingstoke: Macmillan, p. 28.
25. Hume, D. (1953), 'Of the Original Contract', in C. Hendel (ed.), *David Hume's Political Essays*, Indianapolis: Bobbs Merrill, p. 57.
26. Lloyd-Thomas, D. (1995), *Locke On Government*, p. 65.

CHAPTER 4: RECEPTION AND INFLUENCE

1. For an overview of the immediate reception of Locke's *Second Treatise*, see M. Goldie, 'The Reception of Locke', in Goldie. M. and Wokler, R. (2006), *The Cambridge History of Eighteenth-Century Political Thought*, Cambridge: Cambridge University Press, pp. 47–50; and Ashcraft, Richard (1987), *Locke's Two Treatises*, London: Unwin Hyman, pp. 298–305.
2. See Boucher, D. and Kelly, P., 'The Social Contract and its Critics: an overview', in Boucher, D. and Kelly, P. (eds.) (1994), *The Social Contract from Hobbes to Rawls*, London: Routledge, pp. 1–34.
3. Marx, Karl, *The German Ideology*, reprinted in McLellan, David, (ed.) (2004), *Karl Marx: Selected Writings*, Oxford: Oxford University Press.
4. Macpherson, C. B. (1962), *The Political Theory of Possessive Individualism: Hobbes to Locke*, Oxford: Oxford University Press.
5. Dunn, John, 'The Identity of the History of Ideas', in Dunn. J. (1980), *Political Obligation in its Historical Context*, Cambridge: Cambridge University Press.
6. Waldron, Jeremy (2002), *God, Locke and Equality: Christian Foundations in Locke's Political Thought*, Cambridge: Cambridge University Press.
7. Forster, Greg (2005), *John Locke's Politics of Moral Consensus*, Cambridge: Cambridge University Press.
8. Nozick, Robert (1974), *Anarchy, State and Utopia*, Oxford: Basil Blackwell, p. ix.

FURTHER READING

LIFE, TIMES AND POLITICAL CONTEXT

Ashcraft, Richard (1986), *Revolutionary Politics and Locke's Two Treatises of Government*, Princeton: Princeton University Press.

Marshall, John (1994), *John Locke: Resistance, Religion and Responsibility*, Cambridge: Cambridge University Press.

Woolhouse, Roger (2007), *Locke: A Biography*, Cambridge: Cambridge University Press.

LOCKE'S POLITICAL THEORY INTERPRETATIONS

Dunn, John (1969), *The Political Thought of John Locke: an Historical Account of the Argument of the 'Two Treatises of Government'*, Cambridge: Cambridge University Press.

Forster, Greg (2005), *John Locke's Politics of Moral Consensus*, Cambridge: Cambridge University Press.

Grant, Ruth, W. (1987), *John Locke's Liberalism*, Chicago: University of Chicago Press.

Lloyd-Thomas, David (1995), *Locke on Government*, London: Routledge.

Waldron, Jeremy (2002), *God, Locke and Equality: Christian Foundations in Locke's Political Thought*, Cambridge: Cambridge University Press.

Zuckert, Michael, P. (2002), *Launching Liberalism: On Lockean Political Philosophy*, Lawrence: University Press of Kansas.

PRIVATE PROPERTY

Cohen, G. A. (1995), 'Marx and Locke on land and Labour', in *Self-Ownership, Freedom and Equality*, Cambridge: Cambridge University Press.

Kramer, Matthew (1997), *John Locke and the Origins of Private Property*, Cambridge: Cambridge University Press.

Nozick, Robert (1974), *Anarchy, State and Utopia*, Oxford: Basil Blackwell.

Tully, James (1980), *A Discourse on Property: John Locke and his Adversaries*, Cambridge: Cambridge University Press.

Waldron, Jeremy (1988), *The Right to Private Property*, Oxford: Clarendon Press.

WOMEN, PATRIARCHY AND THE FAMILY

Coole, Diana (1993), *Women in Political Theory*, Hemel Hempstead: Harvester Wheatsheaf.

Grant, Ruth (2003), 'John Locke on Women and the Family', in I. Shapiro (ed.), *John Locke Two Treatises of Government and A Letter Concerning Toleration*, New Haven: Yale University Press.

Okin, Susan Moller (1979), *Women in Western Political Thought*, Princeton: Princeton University Press.

Pateman, Carole (1988), *The Sexual Contract*, Cambridge: Polity Press.

CONTRACT AND CONSENT

Beran, Harry (1987), *The Consent Theory of Political Obligation*, London: Croom Helm.

Horton, John (1992), *Political Obligation*, Basingstoke: Macmillan.

Simmons, A. John (1992), *The Lockean Theory of Rights*, Princeton: Princeton University Press.

—— (1993), *On the Edge of Anarchy: Locke Consent and the Limits of Society*, Princeton: Princeton University Press.

DISSOLUTION AND THE RIGHT OF RESISTENCE

Franklin, Julian, H. (1978), *John Locke and the Theory of Sovereignty*, Cambridge: Cambridge University Press.

Simmons, A. John (1993), *On the Edge of Anarchy: Locke Consent and the Limits of Society*, Princeton: Princeton University Press.

BIBLIOGRAPHY

Arblaster, Anthony (1984), *The Rise and Decline of Western Liberalism*, Oxford: Basil Blackwell.

Ashcraft, Richard (1987), *Locke's Two Treatises of Government*, London: Unwin Hyman.

—— (1986), *Revolutionary Politics and Locke's Two Treatises of Government*, Princeton: Princeton University Press.

Ayers, Michael (1991), *Locke: Epistemology and Ontology*, London: Routledge.

Beran, Harry (1987), *The Consent Theory of Political Obligation*, London: Croom Helm.

Boucher, David, and Kelly, Paul, 'The Social Contract and its Critics: an overview', in Boucher, David, and Kelly, Paul (eds) (1994), *The Social Contract from Hobbes to Rawls*, London: Routledge, pp. 1–34.

Chappell, Vere (1994), *The Cambridge Companion to Locke*, Cambridge: Cambridge University Press.

Cohen, G. A. (1995), 'Marx and Locke on land and labour', in *Self-Ownership, Freedom and Equality*, Cambridge: Cambridge University Press.

Coole, Diana (1993), *Women in Political Theory*, Hemel Hempstead: Harvester Wheatsheaf.

Cox, R. H. (1960), *Locke on War and Peace*, Oxford: Oxford University Press.

Cranston, Maurice (1957), *John Locke: a Biography*, London: Longman.

Day, J. P. (1966), 'Locke and Property', *Philosophical Quarterly*, vol. 16, pp. 207–21.

Dunn, John (1969), *The Political Thought of John Locke: an Historical Account of the Argument of the 'Two Treatises of Government'*, Cambridge: Cambridge University Press.

—— 'The Identity of the History of Ideas', in Dunn, J. (1980), *Political Obligation in its Historical Context*, Cambridge: Cambridge University Press.

—— (1984), *Locke*, Oxford: Oxford University Press.

Dworkin, Ronald (1985), *A Matter of Principle*, Oxford: Oxford University Press.

Forster, Greg (2005), *John Locke's Politics of Moral Consensus*, Cambridge: Cambridge University Press.

Franklin, Julian, H. (1978), *John Locke and the Theory of Sovereignty*, Cambridge: Cambridge University Press.

Goldie, Mark, and Wokler, Robert (eds) (2006), *The Cambridge History of Eighteenth-Century Political Thought*, Cambridge: Cambridge University Press.

Gough, John W. (1973), *John Locke's Political Philosophy: Eight Studies*, Oxford: Clarendon Press.

Grant, Ruth, W. (1987), *John Locke's Liberalism*, Chicago: University of Chicago Press.

—— (2003), 'John Locke on Women and the Family', in I. Shapiro (ed.), *John Locke Two Treatises of Government and A Letter Concerning Toleration*, New Haven: Yale University Press.

Harris, Ian (1994), *The Mind of John Locke*, Cambridge: Cambridge University Press.

Harrison, Ross (2003), *Hobbes, Locke and Confusion's Masterpiece*, Cambridge: Cambridge University Press.

Horton, John (1992), *Political Obligation*, Basingstoke: Macmillan.

Israel, Jonathan (2006), *Enlightenment Contested*, Oxford: Oxford University Press.

Kramer, Matthew (1997), *John Locke and the Origins of Private Property*, Cambridge: Cambridge University Press.

Laski, Harold, J. (1996), *The Rise of European Liberalism*, New Brunswick NJ: Transaction Publishers.

Lloyd-Thomas, David (1995), *Locke on Government*, London: Routledge.

Macpherson, C. B. (1962), *The Political Theory of Possessive Individualism*, Oxford: Oxford University Press.

Marshall, John (1994), *John Locke: Resistance, Religion and Responsibility*, Cambridge: Cambridge University Press.

Nozick, Robert (1974), *Anarchy, State and Utopia*, Oxford: Basil Blackwell.

Okin, Susan Moller (1979), *Women in Western Political Thought*, Princeton: Princeton University Press.

Parry, Geraint (1978), *John Locke*, London: George Allen & Unwin.

Pateman, Carole (1988), *The Sexual Contract*, Cambridge: Polity Press.

Rawls, John (1971), *A Theory of Justice*, Cambridge MA: Harvard University Press.

—— (2007), *Lectures on the History of Political Philosophy*, Cambridge MA: Harvard Belknap.

Reeve, Andrew (1986), *Property*, Basingstoke: Macmillan.

Ryan, Alan (1984), *Property and Political Theory*, Oxford: Basil Blackwell.

Seliger, Martin (1968), *The Liberal Politics of John Locke*, London: George Allen & Unwin.

Simmons, A. John (1992), *The Lockean Theory of Rights*, Princeton: Princeton University Press.

—— (1993), *On the Edge of Anarchy: Locke Consent and the Limits of Society*, Princeton: Princeton University Press.

Strauss, Leo (1953), *Natural Right and History*, Chicago: University of Chicago Press.

Tuck, Richard (1979), *Natural Rights Theories*, Cambridge: Cambridge University Press.

Tully, James (1980), *A Discourse on Property: John Locke and his Adversaries*, Cambridge: Cambridge University Press.

—— (1991), 'Locke', *The Cambridge History of Political Thought: 1450–1700*, J. H. Burns and Mark Goldie (eds), Cambridge: Cambridge University Press.

—— (1993), *An Approach to Political Philosophy: Locke in Contexts*, Cambridge: Cambridge University Press.

Waldron, Jeremy (1988), *The Right to Private Property*, Oxford: Clarendon Press.

—— (2002), *God, Locke and Equality: Christian Foundations in Locke's Political Thought*, Cambridge: Cambridge University Press.

Woolhouse, Roger (2007), *Locke: A Biography*, Cambridge: Cambridge University Press.

Zuckert, Michael, P. (1994), *Natural Right and the New Liberalism*, Princeton: Princeton University Press.

—— (2002), *Launching Liberalism: On Lockean Political Philosophy*, Lawrence: University Press of Kansas.

INDEX

Made in the USA
Lexington, KY
15 July 2013